DEEP ECOLOGY AND ANARCHISM
a polemic.

With contributions from Brian Morris, Chris Wilbert, Graham Purchase, Murray Bookchin, Robert Hart, Rodney Aitchtey plus an extract from *Do or Die*, issue ten.

2017 editing and design by
Rob Ray

Printed 1993, 2017

ISBN 978-1-904491-28-6
All applicable rights
reserved

Published by
Freedom Press
84b Whitechapel High St,
London
E1 7QX
freedompress.org.uk

GW00584986

CONTENTS

Can Life Survive?
by Robert Hart   2

a polemic on ecology

Deep Ecology: Not Man Apart
by Rodney Aitchtey   10

Social Ecology, anarchism and Trades Unionism
by Graham Purchase   18

Reflections on "Deep Ecology"
by Brian Morris   31

Deep Ecology, Anarcho-Syndicalism & the Future of Anarchist
Thought
by Murray Bookchin   41

Murray Bookchin's legacy
by Brian Morris   53

The Apple Falls from Grace
by Chris Wilbert   71

after thought, action

Down With Empire, Up With The Spring!
Do or Die Issue Ten   85

Bibliographies   128

References, notes   131

INTRODUCTION

This Freedom Press title originally grew out of issue 17 of *The Raven* journal. At the time discussion of anarchism and the environment was hitting a purple patch which would in short order explode into the popular consciousness through an intense direct action campaign against road building across Britain.

The Earth Liberation Front had been founded here just one year before, Reclaim the Streets was hitting its stride, *Do or Die!* had recently been launched and protests at Twyford Down had shut down the M3 road extension, prompting a mild panic for the government and blanket coverage from national news outlets — the first of many such actions.

As a contribution to the discussions of the day, *deep ecology and anarchism* was able to draw notable writers to give their take on what was already becoming a broad and often chaotic selection of philosophies and ideas.

This volume opens with a challenging contribution "Can Life Survive?" by Robert Hart, a pioneer of forest gardening in the early 1970s and major contributor to the ideas which underpin today's permaculture movement.

His writing is ably followed by contributions from Rodney Aitchey and Graham Purchase, but the core of the book focuses on debate around the thinking of one of the most influential and controversial ecological thinkers of the late 20th century — Murray Bookchin.

Bookchin was an often brilliant and frequently fractious personality whose work mixed elements of libertarian socialism and radical green thinking in ways that often seem common today, but which prompted furious argument at the time. A little over a decade on from his death, for this edition of *deep ecology and anarchism* we include an abridged essay by Brian Morris on the topic of Bookchin's legacy, placed just after an article by Bookchin himself originally written for this collection. Bookchin died in 2006 but has left an enduring legacy with the anarchist movement, one which Morris looks over with the benefit of some distance from those angry rhetorical scuffles which overshadowed the turn of the millennium.

For this edition we also decided to leaven the theory and history with tales of direct action that went on around and after the original publication. Our final essay, "Death With Empire, Up With Spring!" was written for issue ten of *Do or Die!* magazine, printed exactly ten years after *deep ecology and anarchism*. It consists of a historical overview of what was to prove a high point in Britain's environmental direct action movement, from 1991 to 2001.

~ **Rob Ray**

CAN LIFE SURVIVE?
by Robert Hart

Only the indomitable will to survive of ordinary people, coupled with their instinct for mutual aid at times of crisis, can save life on Earth at this most crucial period of world history.

It is useless to put any trust in the powers-that-be. Blinded by their incessant search for short-term profits and petty authority, they will never be induced to take the drastic steps that are essential.

Throughout history, visionaries and prophets, who have cared passionately about the future of the human race, have sought guidance, not from the rich and powerful, but from oppressed and despised minorities.

Only under well-nigh intolerable "marginal conditions," does human nature plumb its full potentialities of inner strength and practical wisdom, that can enable it to pull through against seemingly insuperable odds.

As a young man, the later-to-be anarchist philosopher Peter Kropotkin infuriated his aristocratic father in 1862 by rejecting a life of luxury and ease at the court of St Petersburg in favour of a posting to a military unit in Siberia.

In the then largely unexplored eastern fastnesses of the Russian empire, he sought and found proof of the thesis that mutual aid, rather than conflict and competition, is the crucial factor in evolution.

Similarly, I suggest that famed social figures Mahatma Gandhi, Toyohiko Kagawa and Baba Amte sought out the "lowest of the low," not only out of compassion for their plight, but because they found in them inspiration and encouragement for the colossal regenerative tasks which they were undertaking.

They were establishing new poles by which the dynamics of human development could be regulated. At the present time similar poles of achievement are being set by the women of Africa and the Himalayas who, out of selfless dedication to their families, undertake ever-lengthening and ever more exhausting journeys on foot in search of wood and water.

In both the developmental and environmental spheres, the pendulum swings continually between "North" and "South," the rich world and the poor. "Northern" statesmen, administrators and industrialists see the problems only in the light of charity and population control: how little money they can decently spend on "relief while putting most of the blame on the South for their economic and ecological problems and for not checking the "population explosion."

Such attitudes betray gross ignorance of the true facts. Environmental degradation is overwhelmingly the responsibility of the North: its prodigious emissions of polluting gases and other chemicals, with its wholesale destruction of trees and chemical contamination of soils, combined with its ruthless economic and political exploitation of the South. The North's first duty is not to lecture the South and administer meagre charity, but to get off its back.

If the South were allowed to work out its own salvation, freed from domination, not only by the North, but also by its own North-sponsored dictators and "elites," there is ample evidence that it would find solutions to its economic and ecological problems from which the North could learn valuable lessons.

Despite all the encroachments and invasions of Northern political and economic imperialisms, a characteristic feature of many Southern societies is still the largely self-governing and self-sufficient local community. Such a community provides comprehensive answers to economic, ecological and even population problems.

Bound together by ties of mutual aid, the members have the wisdom and sense of responsibility not to burden their successors with multitudes of mouths that will be unable to be fed. At the same time, the co-operative labour of farming, growing and craftsmanship, often involving music and other cultural activities, together with the natural beauty of the environment, satisfies the inhabitants' emotional and creative urges in ways unimagined by soul-starved Northern city dwellers.

Such communities often exist in remote or difficult areas, rejected by the North as offering sparse or risky financial returns on investment. It is the hardships of life in such areas that strengthen the inhabitants' cohesiveness. The day may well come when many people in the North will be glad to study their survival techniques. Already life in many Northern inner cities is becoming so intolerable that many people are being drawn to adopt "Southern" ways of life. A prospectus for a summer camp in the Shropshire countryside issued by Whose World?, a group with headquarters in Manchester, asks:

Do you believe in the need for a radical transformation of society?
Do you long for a world that's truly equal and just; where we all live sustainably and non-exploitatively; where everyone's needs are met now and always?

It then states the aims of the camp:

✵ To provide all of us who come with an experience of what simple, non-materialistic, communal living — consensus decision-making, trying to look after each other emotionally etc. — could be like and have fun while doing so.

✵ To provide support and encouragement for all of us working towards a vision of a just, sustainable, non-violent way of life.

✵ To build a network of people and communities who want to promote active non-violent resistance and simple, anti-materialist ways of living.

As regards the economic advantages of Third World village communities, many of them satisfy their basic needs, and some even have surpluses for sale, from agroforestry systems that provide an intensity of land-use unknown in the North. Villages in Java, one of the most densely populated rural areas in the world, are surrounded by dense green screens of forest gardens, or pekarangan, in which many of the 500 different species of food plant which the people consume are grown.

These forest gardens provide the best comprehensive, constructive answer to one of today's predominant environmental preoccupations: what to do with the rainforest. Well-meaning Northern environmentalists get very hot under the collar when rainforests are mentioned, asserting forcefully that, at all costs, they must be preserved in toto. But the forests are far too valuable resources to be kept in glass cases.

The tribal peoples who make them their homes have an encyclopaedic knowledge of all the right answers. They know almost every plant and what its uses are. At the same time they use the wild plants to provide shade and shelter for economic crops such as bananas, pineapples and coffee. More than half Tanzania's coffee output is derived from the famous Chagga gardens on the slopes of Mount Kilimanjaro. The forest garden is the world's most advanced system for supplying basic needs, not only food, but fuel, timber, textiles, energy and many other necessities. Agroforestry, in fact, provides the only safe, non-polluting, sustainable answer to the Northern industrialism that is causing such appalling damage to the world's environment, and which is rapidly disintegrating.

In fact, the only comprehensive, constructive answer to both the world's economic and ecological crises is a post-industrial order, which far-sighted Greens have already been advocating for a number of years.

The colossal dangers to all life represented by greenhouse gases, radioactive wastes, CFCs, halons and deforestation will never be overcome by the small-scale piecemeal tinkering measures put forward by statesmen at the Rio conference. Nor will the colossal and ever-increasing suffering caused by poverty, hunger, homelessness, unemployment, violence and avoidable disease be overcome by "market forces," bank loans and IMF-sponsored hydro-electric schemes.

In a world order of which the basic unit would be the small self-sufficient community, meeting most of its essential needs by means of agroforestry, small workshops, and small-scale alternative technology devices, there would be little or no need for road, rail or air transport using polluting fuels. Energy needs would be met by environmentally friendly, non-polluting wind, water, tidal, geothermal, solar and biogas systems. All wastes would be recycled.

Above all, there should be a total ban on the barbarous practice of war, which causes unspeakable damage to the environment as well as untold human suffering. Civilised methods of solving disputes based on reason, mutual respect and psychology, as advocated by religious leaders throughout history, should be developed.

All life on earth could be annihilated by nuclear war as well as by environmental degradation. War never brings lasting solutions to any problem, because it does not eradicate the deep-seated psychological and moral causes of conflict. Imperialistic drives, if suppressed by military action, reappear in economic, political and cultural forms, which do just as much harm to human bodies and minds — in more subtle ways — as does armed conquest. The Second World War has led to a period of environmental destruction, homelessness, human misery, disease, torture, violence, crime and corruption unprecedented in history.

Paul Harrison's (1992) book on the worldwide ecological-economic crisis is called *The Third Revolution*. The three revolutions which he considers crucial to human history are the Neolithic, the Industrial, and the present Environmental Revolution.

The Neolithic Revolution took place when Stone Age man, having developed axes almost as sharp as steel, began his onslaught on his forest home, which has continued with increasing ferocity ever since. Rejecting his hunter-gatherer lifestyle, Neolithic man tried to gain control over his environment by domesticating wild animals and wild crops and thus establishing agriculture. At the same time he developed the crafts of spinning, weaving, pottery and carpentry, and built the first towns.

A little later, war appeared for the first time on the human scene, as did the erosion of upland areas caused by deforestation. Both these trends were greatly intensified by the discovery of metals.

The Industrial Revolution, which began at the beginning of the 18th century, has had infinitely more drastic effects on both human life and the environment. While it has brought great and undeniable benefits in lessening toil, facilitating travel and, above all, in greatly extending the dissemination of information, its wholesale pollution of the environment and use of weapons of mass destruction are totally unacceptable. If human life is to survive beyond the middle of the next century in any tolerable form — or at all — both these features of industrialism must be superseded.

Thus the Environmental Revolution, if it is to succeed, must be as drastic and far-reaching in positive ways, as have the two previous world revolutions in negative ways. It must involve equally radical transformations of life-styles; these cannot be imposed from "above" but must be voluntarily adopted by the people most deeply affected. The motive- power for the Environmental Revolution can only be a worldwide eruption of constructive, non-violent People's Power, comparable to the Gandhian "satya-grahas" in India in the 1920s and 1930s and the overthrow of Communism in Eastern Europe in 1989.

Already there are many indications in many countries that such a movement is building up.

Above all, there is increasing worldwide awareness of the fundamental importance of trees for healing the environment, assuring water supplies, ameliorating the climate, purifying the atmosphere, absorbing CO_2, exhaling oxygen, regenerating degraded soils, stopping erosion — and supplying basic human needs of food, fuel, building materials, textiles, oils and plastics.

A pioneer campaign for the preservation of trees involving People's Power — mainly Women's Power — was launched in the early 1970s in an appallingly degraded sector of the Himalayas.

Called the Chipko ("embrace") movement, it began spontaneously when a group of women embraced trees to prevent them from being felled. From that dramatic start the movement has spread to other parts of India; it has led to a number of official bans on tree-felling and has generated pressure for a more environmentally friendly natural resource policy — the movement continues to inspire activists today.

A tree-planting campaign, also largely involving women, in the Green Belt Movement in Kenya, which has spread rapidly and which its founder, Professor Wangari Maathai, is seeking to extend to 12 other African countries (as of 2017, the movement has planted over 51 million trees).

There are similar campaigns in many other countries. In the Highlands of Scotland, one of the world's many environmental black spots, a campaign is afoot to restore the Great Wood of Caledon, which once covered almost the entire area, and build up a prosperous forest economy, which might absorb many unemployed city-dwellers.

Similar wilderness areas throughout the world — almost all the result of human misuse of the land — could be restored by tree-planting campaigns which could lead to the provision of homes and vital, constructive work for countless millions of homeless, deprived people.

Certain countries, above all, perhaps China and Israel, have demonstrated that even the most arid of deserts can be transformed by trees into areas of fertility, prosperity and beauty. Restoration techniques have been scientifically worked out, involving the planting of drought-resistant trees and shrubs, which provide "nurse conditions" for more delicate trees and other plants supplying fruit and many other economic products and supporting large populations.

The main cause of the ecological crisis is not the "population explosion," as many Northern analysts claim, but gross under-use of the world's land resources.

Apart from totally unproductive deserts, which cover one-third of the earth's land surface, there are vast areas of grassland, much of very poor quality, which is used for grazing cattle and sheep. The average food production of such areas is about half a hundredweight per acre per year. In the Highlands of Scotland it is reckoned that it takes five acres of grassland and moorland to support one sheep. Much of the rest of the world's agricultural land is used for the monocropping of cereals, with an average production of two to four tons per acre per year. But under agroforestry systems annual production exceeding a hundred tons per acre per year is possible. Moreover, under such systems, a wide diversity of food and other useful plants is produced, supplying well balanced diets, as well as fuel, building materials and other necessities.

The food plants produced by an agroforestry system supply the most important factors in human nutrition, in which most diets, in the poor and rich worlds alike, are gravely deficient. These are fruit, whose natural sugars feed the brain and energise the body, and green plants, whose chlorophyll — the basic constituent of all physical life — has a special affinity for the blood. A diet designed for optimum positive health should comprise seventy percent of fruit and green vegetables, preferably consumed fresh and raw.

A disaster afflicting today's world, which is at least as serious as any actual or potential environmental disaster, is the colossal toll of disease caused by bad or inadequate food. The malnutrition of poverty in the Third World is no more drastic in its effects than the malnutrition of affluence in the rich sector — the malnutrition caused by excess of fatty, clogging, over-flavoured and chemically processed foods causes the "diseases of civilisation" which are no less lethal than the diseases caused by destitution and dirt.

Before there can be an Environmental Revolution there must be a Humanistic Revolution. The reason why ever-growing stretches of the earth's surface are hells for human beings, whether they are squalid shanty-towns, polluted and violent inner-city ghettos, squatters" camps, concentration camps or treeless wildernesses, is that the powers who run the world regard people as things, as objects of exploitation or domination. A word coined by Karl Marx in his critique of the capitalist system was *verdinglichung* — "thing-making," though Communist commissars have proved as guilty in this respect as capitalist entrepreneurs. Both groups regard human beings as mere pawns to be used for the furtherance of their personal power and wealth. Similarly, their only interest in a stretch of beautiful countryside is, not how its beauty can be preserved and enhanced, but how most effectively it can be "developed;" whether it can be made to generate more wealth as the site of a building estate, an industrial complex, a factory farm, an airfield, a hydro-electric dam, a nuclear power station, a motorway, or a "theme park."

The attitude of the powers-that-be towards life in its infinite complexity, whether in the form of a human being or a tropical rainforest, is one of gross over-simplification. The human being is only of interest as "consumer," "investor," "labour," "voter," "soldier" or "taxpayer." The forest, with its vast diversity of species, is only of interest as a purveyor of timber, or, burnt to the ground and converted into pasture, as a brief purveyor of hamburgers. The only standard is short-term profit; no regard is paid to longer and wider prospects, to the needs and survival of living beings.

It is among ordinary human beings, not industrial chiefs, bankers, bureaucrats and politicians, that humanistic feelings are found in their greatest intensity. Among our tortured world's supreme needs is the divine commonsense and compassion of the conscientious mother and housewife. This is a manifestation of the power of Gaia, the grassroots dynamic which must supply much of the motive-force of the Environmental Revolution.

Unlike previous revolutions, this must be overwhelmingly non-violent and constructive. It will comprise an ever-increasing profusion of small growing-points, like the new plants that irresistibly spring forth in an area devastated by volcanic eruption.

Already it is possible to detect a multitude of such growing-points in almost every country. A report critical of industrialism was entitled *Limits to Growth*, but no limits should be placed on the growth of new village communities, family farms, organic market-gardens, conservation groups, Green organisations, and co-operative enterprises of all kinds. Even now, the people involved in these must number many millions. If only their efforts could be integrated and co-ordinated into a worldwide New Life Network, they could give rise to a non-governmental organisation which could speak with real authority in the United Nations.

As the primary impulse for all activity comes from the human psyche, the first essential, if mankind is to survive the colossal challenges of the present and future, must be a Moral Revolution. Mutual aid, rather than money, power, status and self-indulgence, must be accepted as the basic law of life. Modern communication technology has forcibly brought home the fact that it is one world. Disasters involving human suffering are shown on television screens with equal immediacy, whether they occur in distant countries or the next street. No longer can people shrug off responsibility for the tribulations of their distant cousins. In fact those tribulations are generally caused by negative or positive factors in the worldwide system and ethos which govern the way the majority of the world's citizens live and work — a system and ethos based on blind selfishness and materialism.

Gandhi said, "There is enough in the world to satisfy everyone's need but not everyone's greed." In fact, the technological know-how exists to give every human being adequate food, water, shelter, clothing, energy and opportunity for self-fulfilment. A worldwide campaign of resource development for need could be a "moral equivalent of war," which would bring deep psychological as well as physical satisfaction to countless millions, not least among those who at present are seeking the soul-destroying "satisfaction" of exploiting, dominating or otherwise hurting their fellow human beings.

Such a campaign, wholly constructive and transcending environmental problems as well as human barriers and rivalries — and involving the planting of trillions of trees — could usher in a period of positive peace and creative activity such as mankind has never known throughout history.

The alternatives face each one of us: a series of ever deepening environmental and economic disasters and conflicts or a world of unprecedented beauty, diversity and abundance.

a polemic on deep ecology

NOT MAN APART
by Rodney Aitchtey

It is the intent of the following essay to shine deep ecology's light onto the question of land itself. Land from which everything emanates.

Philosopher Arne Naess launched the long range international deep ecology movement in Norway in 1972, which attracted the attention of environmental academics worldwide. Awareness grew of just how deep is the deep water in which we are habituated to wallow.

Naess has compared our position to being at the bottom of a well, with our will-power succumbing to the lingering deadly fumes, which would explain the prevalent inertia. Fumes being, apart from insidious vehicle exhausts and airborne pollution, television and advertising.

Pyotr Ouspenskii's prognosis is useful. "All the absurdities and all the contradictions of people, and of human life in general, become explained when we realise that people live in sleep, do everything in sleep, and do not know that they are asleep." Each is a bundle of memories of experiences with some "reserve energy." It is this "reserve energy" which deep ecology taps, and brings to the surface, waking us up.

Deep ecology has become an emotive term and does carry multi-connotations which are like sparks flying from a live terminal, which is as Arne Naess intended. No two people are the same. Deep ecology's philosophy is not rigid, although it does not deviate from Naess' original intention which is to question preconceptions and assumptions until the answer reaches the level of intuition. Something made the American philosopher John Rodman say, in 1978, "It is probably a safe maxim that there will be no revolution in ethics without a revolution in perception."

Naess has said that his vision of deep ecology was awakened by reading a book by Rachel Carson which was published in America in 1962. Her title, Man Against the Earth, was changed to *Silent Spring*. She dedicated the book to Albert Schweitzer in his words: "Man has lost the capacity to foresee and to forestall. He will end by destroying the Earth."

When she had finished writing she sent the manuscript to William Shawn, editor of the New Yorker. His enthusiasm buoyed her into noting, "I knew from his reaction that my message would get across."

While listening to Beethoven's Violin Concerto, "suddenly the tension of four years was broken and I let the tears come... The thoughts of all the birds and other creatures and all the loveliness that is in nature came to me with such a surge of deep happiness, that now I had done what I could — I had been able to complete it." Her book struck home, at people's preconceptions and assumptions, and attempts were made to suppress it. She recalled John Muir (see later) when she said at the end of the book, The "control of nature" is a phrase conceived in arrogance, born of the Neanderthal age of biology and philosophy, when it was supposed that nature exists for the convenience of man.

Arne Naess said of *Silent Spring*, "Rachel Carson went deep and questioned the premises of her society." In 1964, Rachel Carson died. In 1969, Naess resigned as professor in philosophy at the University of Oslo after being there 30 years, so that he could "live rather than function." During his time at the university he had established a name for his work on the philosophies of Baruch Spinoza and Gandhi which he put into practice in direct action in Norway. One of his actions was to pin himself high up to one side of a threatened Norwegian fjord; he refused to descend until plans to build a dam there were dropped, which they were! He was in tune with the lines from this poem by the American poet, Robinson Jeffers (1887–1962):

The Answer
A severed hand
Is an ugly thing, and man disseevered from the earth and stars and his
history ...for contemplation or in fact ...
Often appears atrociously ugly. Integrity is wholeness, the greatest
beauty is
Organic wholeness, the wholeness of life and things, the divine beauty
of the universe. Love that, not man
Apart from that, or else you will share man's pitiful confusions, or drown
in despair when his days darken.

Naess also emphasises "the responsibility of an integrated person to work out his or her reaction to contemporary environmental problems on the basis of a total view."

It is now almost 30 years since *Silent Spring* said "What we have to face is not an occasional dose of poison which has accidentally got into some particle of food, but a persistent and continuous poisoning of the whole human environment." And it was not a new phenomenon then. It has taken centuries to virtually strip the planet of its natural covering.

Five hundred years ago, in 1492, an Italian, Christobal Colón (Columbus) blazed the trail for extermination and environmental destruction up to the present time. He discovered and ravished, where he could, the islands of the West Indies. In 1498, on his third voyage, when he landed on what became Venezuela he took it for another island, until afterwards when natives disabused him. Under the impression he had come upon islands off India he named the natives Indians, which misnomer has stuck onto all the natives of South and North America and Canada. A fellow Italian, Amerigo Vespucci landed up in North America and his first name became attached to the whole continent. There is a statue of him in New York.

In 1992, a statue of Columbus was built in Belgrave Square, London, although no likeness of the man exists. At school I was given the impression he was English. But we are to be Europeanised with its centralised, humanist, materialist values, and Columbus would therefore be seen as a good European to admire.

In the 1780s accounts of the exploits of Columbus and his successors varied so much on the Continent that the learned Abbé Guillaume Raynal decided to assemble the different accounts to find a common thread. It was that they had "harassed the globe and stained it with blood." And the situation has not changed. In Sarawak now a quite horrific extermination process is in force with the destruction of the rainforest. One of the indigenous people recently said, "We are now like fish in the pool of a drying out riverbed." Such distress and death to enable the Japanese to make their fax paper is diabolical.

Ralph Waldo Emerson (1803–1882) in his essay, "Nature," says, "Man is fallen; nature is erect, and serves as a differential thermometer, detecting the presence or absence of the divine sentiment in man." He inspired both Henry Thoreau and John Muir; each in their differing ways put his philosophy into practice. Thoreau, Emerson said, had developed his own thoughts a step further.

Thoreau (1817–1862) urged viewing nature free of preconceptions. Nature became his "society." In his essay "Walking," he said, "... from the forests and wilderness come the tonics and barks which brace mankind." He believed that there would be no regeneration of society without self-reform of the individual. He went to prison in 1848 rather than pay a poll tax because of its going toward the Mexican war effort. In his hut by Waiden pond he put into practice his growing convictions.

John Muir (1838–1914) felt that "One day's exposure to mountains is better than cartloads of books," and he believed that lack of immersion in the natural world was what flawed Emerson's writings.

However, he said of Emerson, "He was as sincere as the trees, his eyes sincere as the sun." Muir was aware of himself going deeper into nature's secrets than Thoreau had been. In 1870 an experience shook him, and he wrote in a letter joyfully, "I'm in the woods woods woods, and they are in me!" He knew that there was no creature higher or lower than another; each had equal right to live and blossom in its own way and own time.

Muir chose to spend most of his life in the mountains, finding comfort among them. Walking was not a word he used for himself; instead, sauntering, with its original sense of musing. Here are words addressed to the boy King Edward VI which show it in use before deep ecological consideration was made to give way to shallowness, losing a sense of rootedness, by the Reformation: " ... do not yourselfe sitt saunteringe alone: as wone that weare in studye most deepe."

Muir's encounters with Indians were reciprocal in admiration. He was given the name Ancoutahan by a band of the Tlingit tribe. A translation might be: revered/learned writer, writing in his notebook; and of them he wrote, "To the Indian mind all nature was instinct with deity. A spirit was embodied in every mountain, stream, and waterfall."

Muir's published studies of natural forces brought him to the notice of the scientific establishment, and he realised that the concern of science was not with the essential oneness of all things, but with breaking down and classification. What frustration he suffered: "When we try to pick out anything by itself we find it hitched to everything else in the universe."

In San Francisco Muir attended some Sunday night sessions with Henry George who was having an influence on early conservation thinking. In *Progress and Poverty* (1879) he suggested that as people had equal rights to breathe the air, so they should to enjoy the earth. He reasoned that whatever man makes or grows is his to do with it as he will.

But, he asks, who made the earth? As it is a "temporary dwelling place" it is not ours to buy or sell, (or despoil). Morally, no man should have more land than that with which he can cope, without exploiting others, and he advocated a Single Tax on undeserved and unearned appreciating income. Marx's wrestle with capital did not go deep enough to touch the earth. He overlooked land, and actually encouraged its exploitation and despoliation. Muir agreed with George that "what has destroyed all previous civilisations has been the conditions produced by the growth of civilisation itself. Henry George was described by President Roosevelt as one of the century's "really great thinkers."

Muir was driven into immediate, frenzied action by a notice signed by three men claiming a valley for themselves to raise livestock. His letter appeared in the *San Francisco Bulletin* in August 1875. It marked the beginning of the concentration of his energies toward defending wilderness from man. Eventually he came up against the commercial conservationists: a deep versus shallow dichotomy. In May 1892, Muir, with sympathetic friends, launched the redoubtable Sierra Club to campaign to preserve the forests and wild features. Muir was elected president and remained so until he died. The National Parks of America owe their existence to Muir's energy. In 1876 he had said, "My life-work is all over the world;" and indeed, the John Muir Trust in Scotland was founded in 1983 with the object of keeping wilderness wild; it is affiliated to the Sierra Club in San Francisco.

And how the Sierra Club for more than three years had to fight the determined attempts of lumbermen and stockmen to cut down nearly half of the Yosemite National Park; they flouted the law, and their 500,000 sheep stripped the earth of meadows and forest.

In 1894, Muir's first book, *The Mountains of California*, roused America to the need for determination to preserve the forests. Serious opposition came from the influential General Land Office. When Muir joined the Forest Commission on a fact-searching inspection, wherever they stopped they found forests cut down and burned, largely by fraudulent means. Muir wrote home, "Wherever the white man goes, the groves vanish."

Roosevelt camped with Muir and told him in a letter afterwards that he had "always begrudged Emerson's not having gone into camp" with him. And after a later visit to California he pronounced on the importance of its water supply: "the water supply cannot be preserved unless the forests are preserved."

In May 1913, Muir was made Doctor of Laws by the president of the University of California who said of him: "John Muir, born in Scotland, reared in the University of Wisconsin, by final choice a Californian, Widely travelled Observer of the world we dwell in, Man of Science and of Letters, Friend and Protector of nature, Uniquely gifted to Interpret unto others Her mind and ways." In 1914 he died. He had said, "A little pure wildness is the one great present want" for people to realise that "Everything is so immeasurably united." *Time Magazine* announced in 1965: "The real father of conservation is considered to be John Muir, a Californian naturalist."

Emerson had absorbed Indian teachings into his writing, Thoreau absorbed Emerson with reservations, Muir likewise and deepened on Thoreau's understanding; then came Aldo Leopold who had absorbed Muir's writings which he had had corroborated by P D Ouspensky's *Tertium Organum*, and his contemporary, Robinson Jeffers, whose influences appear to have been Heraclitus, Spinoza, Schopenhauer, and Nietzsche.

Aldo Leopold (1886–1948) said, "We abuse land because we regard it as a commodity belonging to us. When we see land as a community to which we belong, we may begin to use it with love and respect." His *Land Ethic* is much quoted and appears in Part III, The Upshot, of *A Sand County Almanac*. It was a distillation of nearly half a century of his lifetime spent in forestry and wildlife conservation: "The land ethic simply enlarges the boundaries of the community to include soils, waters, plants, and animals, or collectively: the land."

P D Ouspensky was a contemporary also. Leopold accepted his assurance that there was nothing dead or mechanical in nature; there was life and feeling in everything: a mountain, a tree, a river, the fish in the river, drops of water, rain, a plant, fire — each separately must possess a mind of its own. A section in *Sand County Almanac* is titled "Thinking like a mountain," as is a recent book about deep ecology.

It was also Robinson Jeffers' conviction that the devaluation of human-centred illusions, the turning outward from man to what is boundlessly greater, is the next step in human development; and an essential condition of freedom and of spiritual (i.e. moral and vital) sanity:

Mourning the broken balance, the hopeless prostration of the earth under men's hands and their minds...

He believed human life to be so easy, spent, as it is, thoughtlessly. His poetry delineates "conflict and charity, love, jealousy, hatred, competition, government, vanity and cruelty, and that puerile passion the will to power'.

At the fall of an age men must make sacrifice to renew beauty, to restore strength.

He has been called the poet of inhumanism. Certainly deep ecology is "not man apart" from the earth, taking one beyond that relative thought which separates and competes.

The beauty of things —
Is in the beholder's brain — the human mind's translation of their transhuman
Intrinsic value.

In 1945 John Muir's integral approach was repersonified by David Brower who not only brought Muir to people's minds, but it was found that he had an added attribute: a gift for leadership. An idea of the man is suggested by these words: "It is still a challenge to emulate the freely translated Indian motto, 'where I go I leave no sign'." He became the Sierra Club's first executive director in 1952, and claimed that he looked towards England for her example of National Trust protection of areas of beauty.

Under Brower's leadership the *New York Times* said of the Sierra Club that it had become the "gangbusters of the conservation movement." In 1969 Brower's intransigence removed him from the Sierra Club. He said, "We cannot go on fiddling while the earth's wild places burn in the fires of our undisciplined technology," and he founded Friends of the Earth as well as the John Muir Institute for Environmental Studies.

Honorary deep ecologists such as Thoreau, Muir, Leopold, Carson, Schweitzer, Jeffers and Brower all discovered the shortcomings of the prescribed Christianity, and found space in Eastern philosophy. The Chinese distilled deep Indian thought, and nowhere so aphoristically as in the deep ecological Tao Te Ching. Eastern philosophies aided and aid comprehension and deepen understanding. Otherwise, for Muir, his empathic communion with nature would have found no verbal expression, elliptical in parts as it is!

With so great a history of destruction of the environment as in America it is perhaps not surprising why a consciousness of deep ecology should have infiltrated there as it has. What we know of deep ecology has come through American books, at least until 1989, when Arne Naess' seminal work on deep ecology was published here, thirteen years after it had appeared in Norway: *Ecology, Community and Lifestyle: An Outline of an Ecosophy*. (Eco for earth household and sophy for wisdom). Ecosophical thinking may not be new but Arne Naess has given it a name which has been striking a very deep note, touching the philosophical nerve of the planet in distress.

At this point Edward Carpenter's tombstone can be heard creaking ... *Civilisation, Its Cause and Cure* was published a century ago, also. "Can it be time?"... when "Man will once more feel his unity with his fellows, he will feel his unity with the animals, with the mountains and the streams, with the earth itself and the slow pulse of constellations, not as an abstract dogma of Science or Theology, but as a living and ever present fact."

Naess says, "The essence of deep ecology is to ask deeper questions," to get at the root of truth, not merely the branches and leaves. "We question our society's underlying assumptions. For instance, we can see that instead of an energy crisis we have a crisis of consumption."

Naess' absorption of the Tao Te Ching and Chuang Tzu corroborated his understanding of Spinoza. He was accustomed to regularly retreat to his hut high in the Norwegian mountains, where increasingly he found "contraries indistinguishably blended" (Chuang Tzu). He was getting to the bottom of John Muir's "no mystery but the mystery of harmony."

Chuang Tzu's blending of contraries was nothing other, in the Western mind-frame, than God. The truth dawned as when the first rays of the rising sun embrace the earth. By getting to know nature those glimpses of God, and feeling of being a part of God, grow and deepen. The ultimate, speechless joy can be likened to success after painstaking months, even years, to master a "difficult" musical instrument, and suddenly the purest notes are heard; and there is left only wonder why it eluded one for so long, so simple it has become.

A somersault of the mind, once achieved it is there to stay. For a deep ecologist it is an emotional attachment or expansion of consciousness which underlies being and interrelation with nature. Naess calls it Self-realisation when one's self is widened and deepened. Protection of nature becomes second nature, it becomes naturally protection of one's very own self! Distinctions are overcome: one's self and other cease to be considered as separate. Thus, one identifies with the threatened forest, and acts accordingly.

Without land we would not exist. Without domesticated animals there would be no deserts. The erosion of man's just nature brought with it the erosion of the land. With greed unbounded it is no wonder that we are where we are. The word recession is now bandied about, but not understood for what it is. Material growth is said to be round the corner.

Man did not intend to change the weather, but now that that fact is being acknowledged nothing very much is being done. Profit, like a necklace, must not be tightened, but Capital's self-imposed recession expects everyone to tighten their belts. Reforms are announced which give the impression that something is happening, when nothing is at all.

When Arne Naess led the Norwegian Himalaya Expedition in 1949, he said, "One of the principal objects of the expedition will be to discover at what height the ordinary burner conks out, and how the second functions at greater heights." I would suggest that the ordinary burner, man's suiciding the planet, is conking out, and deep ecology is the second burner.

It is necessary to practise deep ecology with its "total view;" to be self-reliant, rooted in place and nature, simple in means, rich in ends. (Gandhi).

SOCIAL ECOLOGY, ANARCHISM AND TRADES UNIONISM
by Graham Purchase

This essay is a revision of three book reviews published in Rebel Worker between 1989 and 1991.

Part I: Murray Bookchin: The anarchist-ecologist of the late '60s and '70s

Bookchin has deservedly emerged as a major thinker and writer of the late 20th Century. His ideas on the relationship between social ecology, anarchism, and trade-unionism, although controversial and sometimes straightforwardly wrong or dishonest, are nonetheless worthy of our close and considered attention.

Although Bookchin has become openly hostile towards trade-unionism and anarcho-syndicalism, in fact to any class analysis at all, this has not always been the case. Some of his earlier thinking on these subjects, although deeply critical of syndicalism, offered insightful comment upon the value of traditional revolutionary theory and practice, unlike his recent quite unnecessary attacks on anarchism. His essay *Self-management and the New Technology*, written in 1979 is perhaps most important in this respect. In this essay Bookchin argues that the syndicalist conception of the "factory" or the "workplace" as being of overriding importance as a focus for political and social activity in a future anarchist society is an overly optimistic view of the liberatory potential of large- scale industrial activity. Bookchin claims the factory has destroyed the craftsman and the artisan and degraded the nature of work and labour through relying on a system of mass-industrial production that reduces human beings to mere engine parts:

> Of the technical changes that separate our own era from the past ones no single device was more important than that of the least mechanical of all — the factory. Neither Watt's steam engine nor Bessemer's furnace was more significant than the simple process of rationalising labour into an industrial engine for the production of commodities. Machinery, in the conventional sense of the term, heightened this process vastly — but the systemic rationalisation of labour to serve in ever specialised tasks demolished the technical structure of self-managed societies and ultimately of workmanship — the "selfhood" of the economic realm ... True craftsmanship is loving work, not onerous

toil. It arouses the senses, not dulls them. It adds dignity to humanity, not demeans it. It gives free range to the spirit, not aborts it. Within the technical sphere it is the expression of selfhood par excellence — of individuation, consciousness, and freedom. These words dance throughout every account of well-crafted objects and artistic works.

The factory worker lives merely on the memory of such traits. The din of the factory drowns out every thought, not to speak of any song; the division of labour denies the worker any relationship to the community; the rationalisation of labour dulls his or her senses and exhausts his or her body. There is no room whatever for any of the artisan's modes of expression — from artistry to spirituality — other than an interaction with objects that reduce the worker to a mere object ... Marxism and syndicalism alike, by virtue of their commitment to the factory as a revolutionary social arena, must recast self-management to mean the industrial management of the self ... Both ideologies share the notion that the factory is the "school" of revolution and in the case of syndicalism, of social reconstruction, rather than its undoing. Most share a common commitment to the factory's structural role as a source of social mobilisation ... The factory not only serves to mobilise and train the proletariat but to dehumanise it. Freedom is to be found not within the factory but outside it.

~ *Towards an Ecological Society*,
Black Rose Books, 1980, pp 123–6 passim

Bookchin concludes that the factory system upon which industrial syndicalism rests, is intrinsically authoritarian and dehumanising. The syndicalists have confused the factory, the "realm of economic necessity," with the "realm of social freedom," which is nature, wilderness, community and the liberated city. Contrary to the syndicalist vision, the factory could not on any account ever be regarded as the primary locus of political action and freedom. Only the re-emergence of a freely communicating, non-hierarchical and economically-integrated social existence would be genuinely capable of guaranteeing liberty and prosperity. Besides, Bookchin later argues, the coal-steel-oil technology upon which the factory system was based is economically redundant, through resource depletion. Solar and wind energies etc., although capable of being used in large scale industrial manufacturing processes, are much more efficiently applied on a local or small scale basis. An economic infrastructure consisting of a large number of much smaller workshops producing individually crafted tools from local non-polluting power sources, within the context of an ecologically integrated community, not only represented a truly ecological vision of human social destiny, but one that also saw no need for the vast and intrinsically dehumanising industrial manufacturing plants and factories of a past era. The factory no longer represented even the realm of necessity — environmental determinants having rendered the factory system of industrial production ecologically and vis a vis economically redundant.

Bookchin in this penetrating essay makes fair comment. The pictures that have until recently adorned our anarcho-syndicalist journals — of thousands of workers, heads held high and anarchist banners in hand, marching out of rows of factories triumphantly belching out black smoke in unison — exhibit a singular inability to appreciate the scope and challenge of the ecological revolution that threatens to engulf both anarchisms alike. The reasons for this are historical and practical and are not due to any theoretical shortcomings. At the end of the 19th century, which witnessed rapid industrial development (a peasantry, an urban proletariat, and a Marxist and socialist opposition that regarded the ecological and anarchist ideal of eco-regional self-sufficiency and town/ country balance as too utopian, or as indicative of a backward looking, pre-industrial ideology), anarchism and anarchists as an organised political force saw fit, and with good reasons, to devote a substantial amount of its efforts towards industrial and trades-unions activity and downplay the more ecological aspects of the anarchist vision. This was an eminently practical response to the organisational problems of the day and anarcho-syndicalists through no fault of their own have tended to focus upon industrial democracy within the factory or yard and have to some extent ignored other, wider ecological aspects of the anarchist tradition.

Anarchism however, unlike Marxism, has always taken a profound interest in the proper relationship of industry to ecology (most famously exhibited in Kropotkin's *Fields, Factories & Workshops*) and Bookchin has in response to our current ecological concerns been quite correct in stressing the importance of the ecological region, green technology and ecologically integrated cities and communities within anarchist theory and thereby restore a proper sense of balance to the anarchist and ecological debate.

This essay was however written over a decade ago and with the other essays in *Towards an Ecological Society* in which it is anthologised forms a bridge between the two phases of his writing and thinking: Bookchin the anarchist-ecologist of the 1960s and '70s and Bookchin the social ecologist of the 1980s and '90s. Bookchin the social ecologist is far less kind on anarchism and trades unionism than he might otherwise be. Bookchin has without doubt been one of the most prominent anti-Statist thinkers of recent decades. His two pamphlets *Ecology and Revolutionary Thought* and

Towards a Liberatory Technology (both written in 1965 and reprinted in an anthology of his writings from the period entitled *Post Scarcity Anarchism*) are clear, succinct, and easily understandable statements of the ecological-anarchist viewpoint displaying all the most admirable aspects of anarchist pamphleteering and collectively representing some of the best and most important radical writings of the 1960s. Bookchin in these early pamphlets as well as his two later books; *The Limits of the City* (1974) and *Toward an Ecological Society* (1980) brought up to date and enlarged upon many of the social-ecological insights and ideas to be found in the works of past anarchist thinkers (Fourier, Peter Kropotkin and Elisée Reclus) clearly, logically and convincingly showing that anarchism with its non-centralist and non-hierarchical philosophy envisioning a harmonious stateless order composed of federation of self-governing cities ecologically integrated with their surrounding bio-regions is the only social philosophy capable of ensuring the long-term survival of both our species and our planet. Most of the above mentioned works were however written nearly two decades ago and since the end of the 1970s Bookchin has spent his time expounding his "self-styled" ecological philosophy — social ecology — publishing many books on the subject; *The Ecology of Freedom* (1982), *The Modern Crisis* (1986), *Remaking Society* (1989) and *The Philosophy of Social Ecology* (1990).

Part II: Bookchin, the social ecologist of the '80s and '90s

Although none of the basic tenets of Bookchin's theory of social ecology are in anyway incompatible with social-anarchism and although not denying the importance of anarchism, in his more recent works he rarely mentions the word, and then only in passing. His explicit rejection of "working class organisation" and "trade unions" shows a widening emotional and philosophical gap between his theory of social ecology with the traditions of anarchism.

None the less, many things that Bookchin has to say about a range of issues are relevant to anarchism and anarchists. This is especially true of his extended discussions on the role of patriarchy in creating a hierarchical, exploitative and anti-ecological social system which are valuable and explore issues, somewhat underplayed by Kropotkin and Emma Goldman in their analysis of the evolution and maintenance of authoritarian structures in human society. (Reclus however in the way he uses gender ascription, he and she, about nature is more interesting in this respect than otherwise supposed.) It is in his rejection of class analysis, however, that Bookchin really seeks to form a cleavage between anarchism and his favoured theory of social ecology. In the most accessible of his recent works, *The Modern Crisis*, his attacks on anarchism, the IWW and trades-unionism are simply outrageous.

Anarchism, claims Bookchin, because of its insistence upon class analysis and a belief in the overriding revolutionary importance of the industrial proletariat, represents with Marxism just another tired old socialist philosophy which is no longer relevant to the present day:

'The politics we must pursue is grassroots, fertilised by the ecological, feminist, communitarian and anti-war movements that have patently displaced the traditional workers' movement of half a century ago. Here the so called revolutionary ideologies of our era — socialism and anarchism — fall upon hard times. Besides, their "constituency" is literally being "phased out." The factory in its traditional form is gradually becoming an archaism. Robots will soon replace the assembly line as the agents of mass industrial production. Hence future generation of industrial proletarian may be a marginal stratum marking the end of US industrial society.

> The new "classless class" we now deduce is united more by cultural ties than economic ones: ethnics, women, countercultural people, environmentalists, the aged, unemployables or unemployed, the "ghetto" people, etc. It is this "counterculture" in the broadest sense of the term with its battery of alternative organisations, technologies, periodicals, food co-operatives, health and women's centres that seems to offer common resistance to Caesarism and corporatism. The re-emergence of "the people" in contrast to the steady decline of "the proletariat" verifies the ascendancy of community over factory, of town and neighbourhood over assembly line. The hand fits the glove perfectly — and clenched it makes the real fist of our time.
>
> ~*The Modern Crisis*, Ch.4, passim

Exactly what sense are we to make of such sweeping dismissals of several centuries of sustained resistance to the encroachments of capital and state by ordinary working people is quite unclear. Anarchism and anarcho-syndicalism have to my knowledge always emphasised the need to foster community and has never made the absurd claim that society could be "organised from the factory floor." The primary unit of anarchist society has always been the free, ecologically integrated city or town — how else could one hope to organise social life in the absence of the nation-state? Besides, in the absence of state-supported industrial capitalism trades unions and workers' co-operatives — be they bakers, grocers, coach builders, postal workers or tram drivers would seem to be a quite natural, indeed logical and rational way of enabling ordinary working people to co-ordinate the economic and industrial life of their city, for the benefit of themselves rather than for the state or a handful of capitalist barons and it is simply dishonest of Bookchin to claim that anarchism has emphasised the historical destiny of the industrial proletariat at the expense of community and free city life. Beyond this, trade unions are composed of people — feminists, peace activists and ecologists included and are simply a means by which people can come to organise their trade or industry in a spirit of equality, peace and co-operation.

Although thankfully, tens of millions of people are no longer forced to claw at rock with crude picks in the bowels of the earth I fail to see why Bookchin is confident that the "worker" is an obsoletion. How is one to travel or phone another city in Bookchin's ideal world of liberated, self- sufficient city-communes unless we have to repair the roads, railway or telephone cables? People will always wish to direct objects through organised space and hence a postal service will always be necessary (if we ever come to colonise other planets even more necessary). Economic and industrial life is unfortunately global in nature and the idea that one could organise an inter-continental railway network from the individual town or city is as absurd as the proposition that one could organise social life from the factory floor — an idea that he mistakenly credits to industrial-syndicalism.

The industrial proletariat, although it may certainly never represent the force of numbers that it did a century ago is hardly likely to disappear and anarchism simply states that in the absence of capitalism and the nation state the workers in each industry must organise their affairs for the good of themselves, their city, their ecological region and the whole of humanity. Anarchism is not a worker's party — it is an idea that embraces all manifestations of human social life — the free city, the agricultural collective, the hobby group and trades-unions in so far as they are useful to our species and operate freely of government in a non hierarchical manner.

Bookchin is more constructive when he points to the "green-network" as providing a new and significant springboard to revolutionary transformation.

Over the past 30 years, individuals and groups of people connected by nothing else than a love of the Earth have set about putting their philosophies into action upon a local basis. Local groups of horticulturalists growing native trees for free distribution, organic food co-operatives, forest action groups and a plethora of specialised ecological journals and zines, etc., bringing people together from all backgrounds, races and classes. The local, popular decentralised nature of this green networking representing a powerful and non-centralised force in the direction of social and ecological change.

At the more radical end of the green-network there are people who care deeply about the environment but have become disillusioned about the ability of the state/capitalist order to solve the urgent ecological problems of the day and have set out in the name of common-sense and humanity to save the planet by any reasonable means — legal or otherwise. These people have flung themselves in front of bulldozers and rainforest timber ships. Their antics and exploits have undoubtedly captured the popular imagination and these people have thankfully had comparative success in saving significant portions of wilderness from destruction. Due however to the lack of a significant working class power base their efforts have resulted in them having won few battles at the price of rapidly losing the ecological war. They didn't get their message across to their potentially most powerful and effective ally — trades-unions and the organised working classes. Capitalism and the state which have undoubtedly been the cause of untold environmental destruction has been fought for centuries by working class organisations inspired by a vision of more equal, just and equitable society. The fact that capitalism and state are not only unjust and authoritarian but also extremely environmentally destructive only seeks to confirm the inherent correctness of centuries of radical working class organisation and trades-union opposition to the encroachment of capitalism and the military state upon the social and ecological fabric of human society. The heroic and consistent effort of working class organisation to resist state-sponsored capitalist exploitation is a long and bloody history involving the useless murder, ruthless torture of millions upon millions of ordinary people whose only crime was to attempt to protect their communities and their natural resources from being sacrificed for the short-term benefit of the rich and powerful.

Eco-activists are relative newcomers to the art of organised resistance to the capitalist and military state and have yet to digest the hard historical fact that the institution of state-sponsored multi-national exploitation cannot be defeated without the commitment of large sections of the organised working classes to the green cause. It is the working classes who transform raw nature (trees, minerals, etc.) into the industrial products we consume — and regardless of the wishes of government, or their capitalist masters, are ultimately capable of initiating change.

The tragic lack of communication between eco-activist groups and trades unions has meant that the ecology movement has suffered from a significant lessening of its practical power-base and has led to the absurd situation in Australia of green activists fighting with rank-and-file members of logging-unions, whose members, history has shown us, have little to gain from large scale exploitation of primary forest land.

The attempted assassination of IWW/Earth First! organisers in the US should serve as a lesson for both the greenies and the workers alike — that the real enemy are the institutions of capital and state and not one another. Both the greenies and the working class would be better served by joining together and working towards a grass-roots, revitalised and ecologically informed trades-union movement which if not capable (for the time being) of overthrowing the state-military forces of the rich and powerful is at least able to resist the worst excesses of the present profoundly destructive state-capitalist order. That the welfare of the worker is intimately dependent upon a healthy environment is an unquestionable fact, and both eco-activists and trade-unionists must choose the path of strength and victory by striving to achieve ever greater levels of co-operation and common purpose within and between their respective organisations.

I have encountered thousands of people who on a local and co-operative basis are constructively working towards a greener future — there are however many intellectually degenerate and philosophically idiotic concepts contained within the "green ideology" that holds many of these people together — Earthworshipping, rituals, astrology and eco-mysticism, etc. which tend to make for a less than coherent green movement. The bourgeois or middle class element has further weakened the practical worth of many of the more successful "green" ventures of recent years (e.g. The Body Shop). Expensive health food shops and trendy bookshops selling a wealth of over-priced environmental paraphernalia reveal more a love of profit — an ability to "catch on" to a new idea rather than a genuine and unimpeded love of nature. Lacking in class consciousness the green movement has all too easily let itself be integrated with the capitalist system and is therefore caught in an intellectual and tactical contradiction. Its members, predominantly coming from bourgeois background, are unable to be truly critical of the inherently destructive and anti-ecological aspects of the capitalist and class system of which they uncritically form a part.

Large sections of the "green movement" take a simplistic and anti-technological stance. Industrialism as such and not industrial being seen as a curse of humanity and nature. Other sections of the anarchist and green movement take a more sophisticated position about technology and insist upon the fact that there has been a second industrial revolution — the communications, computer and technological revolution which has a life of its own that may have superseded its origins in capitalism and which threatens to wreak ever-greater levels of social and ecological disintegration. Whether the technological revolution will yield predominantly libertarian or authoritarian results is of course a matter of speculation — and only time will tell. But Bookchin in advocating both craftsmanship and large industrial plants run by robots seems confused on the issue! Bookchin has never to my knowledge ever endorsed any kind of anti-technological viewpoint — that makes his anti-union stance all the more puzzling! How is one to design, implement, manufacture and recycle in a non-authoritarian and co-operative manner the environmentally friendly eco-technologies to which he so frequently refers unless he is willing to enter dialogue with the industrial proletariat who form the backbone of the profoundly destructive oil-steel-coal culture of the present day, but whose force of strength and brute labour could turn ammunitions factories into wind generator manufacturing plants and our forests into gardens, undreamt of by the prophets of all ages? The need to move away from large-scale industrial activity is obvious to the ecologist — but our present factories must begin to design, manufacture and distribute the new technologies of tomorrow. A successful end to this period of transition and technological scale readjustment towards the decentralised application of agro-industrial production cannot be achieved without the co-operation of the industrial proletariat.

Undeterred, Bookchin goes on to insult US anarchists and trade unionists of the past. "These immigrant socialists and anarchists (presumably referring to such people as Emma Goldman or Alexander Berkman) were largely unionists rather than revolutionary utopians" who had little understanding of American democratic traditions. Had the American people ignored the "narrow" and "class based" ideologies of these anarchist and socialist foreigners and upheld the individualistic values of the American Constitution — concretely enshrined in the small town meetings of the pioneers — an authentic American radicalism could have taken a firmer root and the confederal and decentralised vision of a free-American republic could well have become a reality:

Irish direct action, German Marxism, Italian anarchism and Jewish socialism have always been confined to the ghettos of American social life. Combatants of a pre-capitalist world, these militant European immigrants stood at odds with an ever-changing Anglo-Saxon society ... whose constitution had been wrought from the struggle for Englishmen's Rights, not against feudal satraps. Admittedly these "rights" were meant for white men rather than people of colour. But rights they were in any case — universal, "inalienable rights" that could have expressed higher ethical and political aspirations than the myths of a "workers' party" or the day dream of "One Big Union" to cite the illusions of socialists and syndicalists alike.

Had the Congregationalist town-meeting conception of democracy been fostered ... and the middle classes been joined to the working classes by a genuine people's movement instead of being fractured into sharply delineated class movements it would be difficult to predict the innovative direction American social life might have followed. Yet never did American radicals, foreign born or native, ask why socialist ideas never took root outside the confines of the ghettos, in this, the most industrialised country in the world.

~ *The Modern Crisis*
Ch 4 passim

Again what sense is one to make of such comments? Bookchin accuses American radicals of the past of having a ghetto outlook — yet it is precisely this group of people, "ethnics, unemployables and the ghetto people" whom Bookchin underlined in the previously quoted passage as representing the new revolutionary "classless class" of people who will somehow organise the co-operative suburban communities of the future social ecological order. Interestingly the "ethnic, unemployable and ghetto people" of the 19th century of whom he speaks so disparagingly found the best way to overcome their difficulties was to form themselves into unions on the basis of location, culture, trade and interest and collectively fight in One Big Union of ordinary people for a more just and equitable world.

Besides the specific organisation to which he refers, the IWW was not unappealing to "native" Americans as Bookchin suggests — rather they were systematically smashed in a most brutal fashion by the combined forces of federal military might, and the black plantation workers of America's deep south who were organised at great risk to life by IWW representatives had little stake in the comfortable middle-class vision of small town life of which Bookchin speaks. Moreover the IWW who counted both lesbians and Red Indian organisers amongst its ranks was the first union to call for equal pay and conditions for women and actively sought to set up unions for prostitutes — and in doing so achieved far more for the feminist cause than any amount of theorising about the evolution of patriarchy could ever hope to have done.

Finally anarchism in embracing trades-unionism did not, as Bookchin claims, have some naive or mythical faith in the ability of working class culture to save the world. Anarchism did not look towards the Marxist vision of a worker's paradise; it merely said that working people if they wanted to create a more balanced and equitable world they must join together and organise for themselves. Trades unionists which were then, as now, capable of bringing millions of workers together in the general strike was not an end in itself but rather a vehicle for putting ideas into action and produce movement capable of resisting the military might and economic imperialism of the state-capitalist power monopoly.

Groups of peace protesters or environmentalists singing songs outside nuclear bases, although not irrelevant or unproductive, do not by themselves represent an organisational basis for sustained resistance to the state-capitalist system on a country-wide basis, as Bookchin claims. Unless the telephones, railways, and other vital industrial systems continue to function from the moment the state-capitalist order begins to crumble, then all Bookchin's ideas concerning an ecologically integrated and decentralised republic in the absence of the state (i.e. anarchism) will remain nothing but a pipe-dream.

The overly aggressive industrial culture which has led our planet to the brink of catastrophe must certainly undergo radical changes, but this in no way implies that industrial unionism should disappear. On the contrary, an ecologically informed and regenerated trade union movement could do much to initiate the necessary changes. The boycotting of environmentally damaging substances and industrial practices; the insistence on doing healthy work in an environmentally sustainable manner; of producing socially necessary products based on need rather than profit; etc., are real issues, capable of being forced home by traditional means. Strikes, walk-outs, and sabotage would undoubtedly bring about the changes in our industrial infrastructure quicker than environmental legislation and any number of health food stores. For instance, the Green Bans. In fact the tragic failure of the green movement to get their message across to ordinary workers and union members, has resulted in a significant lack of power for both parties. Bookchin's comments are at best unconstructive and at worst positively harmful.

Further evidence of Bookchin's attempt to distance himself and his theory of social ecology from anarchism can be seen in his latest book, The Philosophy of social ecology (1990) in which he attempts to provide an abstract philosophical basis for his social-ecological theories.

Depressingly, the rich ecological content contained in anarchist life-philosophy is largely unacknowledged — and although Bookchin regards an anti-hierarchical, non-centrist, self-determining and freely evolving concept of nature and society as both rational and desirable — anarchism a rich intellectual source of many of these ideas in terms of both its theory and practice is dealt with in a few paragraphs in a token, shallow and unconvincing manner. Instead Bookchin presents us with an intellectual history of the development of social-ecological thought which sees fit to devote pages upon pages to Diderot's "sensibilities" and Hegel's "Concept of Spirit" at the expense of Kropotkin's ethical naturalism, Reclus' bioregionalism or Fourier's ecological-utopianism — all of which (as Bookchin well knows) contain important truths and insights and have made a significant contribution to the development of his own social- ecological thinking. Instead, the book, which is subtitled *Essays on Dialectical Naturalism*, informs those readers who wish to find out more about the philosophical basis of social ecology and ecological ethics to study the notoriously cloudy pages of Hegel's *Phenomenology of Spirit.*

What has led to Bookchin's disillusionment with the organised anarchist movement is of course a matter of speculation. A generous explanation of his objectives is that he wishes to produce an ecological ethics and philosophy that does not scare people off through using the emotionally loaded and popularly misunderstood term "anarchy" whilst integrating the more anarchistic ideas and elements floating around in the peace, environmentalist and feminist movements within a broadly anti-Statist framework. If this is indeed his intention then he has, in my opinion been quite successful. His theory of social ecology is presented in a rational, scientific and secular format that can enter dialogue in a meaningful way with other bodies of thought in the western philosophical tradition.

The misrepresentations of anarchist theory and practice do however perhaps require a less generous assessment of Bookchin's motives, unconscious or not, that goes beyond the not-uncommon fault of having an insatiable appetite for controversy. Bookchin is a gifted and talented writer and thinker, the value and intellectual credibility of his work may however be coming increasingly undermined by an unhealthy desire to be the intellectual leader and founder of a "new" ecological movement. The sole modern originator of the bundle of ideas he had chosen to call social ecology.

Although to be fair Bookchin does acknowledge the influence of the great anarchist theoretician and bio-geographer in all the above mentioned works, he does so only in passing and certainly exhibits no real desire to deal with Kropotkin's thought in the detail and at the length it deserves. There are of course no real developments in social and political theory. The battles between nature and society, freedom and tyranny, liberty and authority etc., have been with us since the beginning of human-time and Kropotkin no more than Bookchin can claim to have originated the libertarian and anarchist debate.

Nonetheless, with the possible exception of his analysis of the development of patriarchy (and Reclus' concepts of the organic, complementary nature of the man-woman-nature relationship are in many ways similar to Bookchin's) all of the basic components of Bookchin's social-ecological vision — diversity, decentralisation, complementarity, alternative technology, municipal-socialism, self-sufficiency, direct-democracy — were fully elaborated in the works of the great anarchist thinkers of the past — Charles Fourier, Elisée Reclus and Peter Kropotkin — all of whom advocate a global federation of autonomous and ecologically integrated cities and towns — and Bookchin has done little more than update these ideas and present them in a modern form. A task I might say that is no small achievement and one that he has performed admirably.

To be sure anarchism in common with most other movements and practices has much to gain from incorporating the insights of feminist analysis of the development of authority and hierarchy into its vision of a social and ecologically harmonious society — and Bookchin in attempting to integrate a broadly socialist-feminist perspective with anarchist principles has done much valuable work in recent years. Many viewpoints contained in the socialist-feminist analysis of history and society, have however, always existed (though latently) within the anarchist movement, and anarchism is considerably less guilty of having ignored women's issues than most other social protest movements of the recent past. To use socialist-feminist ideas on hierarchy, authority and the state and blend them with concepts within the broader anarchist tradition, as Bookchin has done, although necessary, is not a particularly exacting intellectual task. Literally to filch all the major ecological insights of anarchist theory and practice, superficially dress them up in a socialist-feminist cum neo-Hegelian garb and go on to more or less claim them as his own is reprehensible. To actively misrepresent the movement from where these ideas originally came is to exhibit an intellectual schizophrenia and commit an intellectual outrage.

> Like Gresham's Law, not only does bad money drive out good, but futuristic "scenarios" will destroy the utopian dimension of the revolutionary project. Never in the past has it been so necessary to retain the utmost clarity, coherence, and purposefulness that is required of our era. In a society that has made survival, adaptation, and co-existence a mode of domination and annihilation, there can be no compromises with contradictions — only their total resolution in a new ecological society or the inevitability of hopeless surrender.
>
> **Murray Bookchin**
> *Toward an Ecological Society*

REFLECTIONS ON "DEEP ECOLOGY"
by Brian Morris

A couple of years ago George Bradford wrote a lucid and trenchant critique of "deep ecology" in a pamphlet entitled *How Deep is Deep Ecology*.[1] It was specifically aimed at the deep ecology espoused by writers like Bill Devall, George Sessions and Dave Foreman, and it echoed many of the criticisms earlier voiced by Murray Bookchin.[2] Both Bradford and Bookchin essentially challenge the biocentric approach of the deep ecologists — which entails the notion of "biospecies equality" This in essence was the deep ecologists" answer to the anthropocentrism so dominant in Western culture, anthropocentrism being the idea that humans are separate from, and superior to the rest of nature, and that this therefore justified using nature simply as a resource. What Bradford and Bookchin suggest is that the deep ecologists simply replicate (and inverse) the opposition between humans and nature. But whereas the advocates of the Promethean ethic imply the control and domination of nature by humans, contemporary deep ecologists, many of them acolytes of "natural law" theory, have an insidious image of a humanity that is "dominated by nature." Such "anti-humanism" Bookchin and Bradford feel is perverse, unecological, and at extremes leads to misanthropy. The idea that humans should "obey" the "laws of nature" is an idea that they both seriously challenge. And they go on to suggest that by focusing entirely on the category "humanity" the deep ecologists ignore, or completely obscure, the social origins of ecological problems. The notion that African children should be left to starve because they are over-populating the continent, that disease is a natural check on humans and helps to maintain the "balance of nature," that "immigrants" to the United States should be kept out because they threaten "our" resources — all advocated by deep ecology enthusiasts in a rather Malthusian fashion — are all discussed and refuted by Bookchin and Bradford. Such biocentrism and anti-humanism, they argue, is both reactionary and authoritarian in its implications, and substitutes a naive understanding of "nature" for a critical study of real social issues and concerns. Bradford sums it up by suggesting that the deep ecologists "have no really "deep" critique of the state, empire, technology and capital, reducing the complex web of human relations to a simplistic, abstract, scientistic caricature" (p10). Bookchin of course argues that the ecological crisis is not caused by an undifferentiated "humanity" but by the capitalist system, which has reduced human beings to mere commodities, destroyed the cultural integrity of many "Third World" communities, and, via corporate interests, has caused devastation and deterioration of the natural world — through deforestation, monoculture, and pollution.

In response to the criticisms of the social ecologists several deep ecologists, like Warwick Fox and Judi Bari, have suggested that Bookchin still retains an "anthropocentric" outlook, and that the "left" have no vision of an ecological society — a suggestion that indicates either a woeful ignorance or, alternatively, a slanderous misinterpretation of what Bookchin has been advocating for over three decades.

The polemical exchanges between the deep and social ecologists have been very much a part of the radical ecology scene in the United States over the past decade — in contrast to the ecology scene in Britain where the likes of Jonathon Porritt, a genteel reformer, seem to get the media prominence. But this debate took an important twist in May 1989 when Dave Foreman was arrested by the FBI. An ecological activist who advocates non-violent direct action to protect wilderness areas and rainforests, Foreman had been one of the founders of the "Earth First!" group. Over the years this group had been infiltrated by US government informers and agent provocateurs seeking to entrap the ecological activists into illegal activities. Foreman was dragged out of his bed by armed FBI men one dawn and charged with conspiracy to damage government property. Six months later Murray Bookchin and Dave Foreman came together for a public debate, to discuss their differences, and to defend the integrity of the radical ecology movement. What came out of this debate is that whereas Foreman had largely taken to heart the criticisms of deep ecology — and had become a staunch "anti-capitalist" and had withdrawn many of his more extreme anti-humanist statements — Bookchin continued to reiterate with stridency the kind of social ecology that he had been advocating and developing over the years — and thus came to argue for a "new politics," the need for a social movement that can effectively resist and ultimately replace both the nation-state and corporate capitalism. He admitted that he had no pat formulas for making such a revolution, but questioned the feasibility of a reformist strategy, one that merely sets its sights on "improving" the current system of power and inequality.[3]

What is of interest about these various debates is that the figure of Arne Naess, who is alleged to be the founder and the "inspiration" behind the "deep ecology" movement tends to hover only in the background. Naess is discussed by writers like Devall,[4] but though deep ecology itself has had media prominence, its founder is very much a marginal scholar. A couple of years ago I scoured the bookshops in London looking for something on, or by, Arne Naess and drew a complete blank. Happily his important study *Ecology, Community and Lifestyle*[5] has now been translated from the Norwegian, and this gives us an opportunity to assess the thoughts of a philosopher the deep ecologists pay homage to, but whose own ideas remain largely unknown outside his own country and a narrow circle of deep ecology enthusiasts.

Arne Naess is a Norwegian philosopher and mountaineer who has spent most of his life teaching philosophy in academia. His particular interests were semantics and the philosophy of science, and in the 1930s he appears to have been associated with the logical positivists — whose philosophy stands in stark contrast to Naess" present views. Naess has published important studies of Gandhi and Spinoza, and the influence of these two contrasting figures is clearly apparent in his work. His whole mode of presentation — abstract, normative and geometric — as well as his philosophy — in seeing self-realisation as involving "identification" with nature — has affinities with that of Spinoza. Indeed he summarises his own philosophy on one page (209), with an abstract schema of numbered boxes all neatly and logically linked by a series of lines, hanging together like a frozen mobile. Anything less organic it would be hard to imagine, but it reminds one of the gentle Spinoza.

Naess calls his own philosophy of deep ecology "Philosophy T" — the suggestion being that what he presents in the book is his own unique philosophy, named after a mountain hut in Norway, Tvergastein. (Without Naess is a ghost writer who would have thought otherwise?) The implication of this, however, is his insistence that everyone should work out their own philosophy and develop, through reflection and action, their own system of thought. Like many contemporary writers — and in this Naess is offering little that is original — Naess stresses the gravity of the present ecological situation — the environmental deterioration and devastation that is taking place on an ever-increasing scale due to the present system of production and consumption, and to the lack of any adequate policies regarding human population increase. This ecological crisis Naess suggests can only be countered by a "new renaissance," by a "new path" with new criteria for "progress, efficiency and rational action" — Naess strangely retaining some of the key terms of the market economists and of capitalist ideology. This leads Naess to make a clear distinction between "deep" and "shallow" ecology — which he first introduced in an article in 1973 — the latter being a reformist attitude to the present ecological crisis, one that still retains a utilitarian, anthropocentric approach to nature, and does not suggest any fundamental change to the present economic system. This distinction is similar to that long ago made by Bookchin who contrasted "environmentalism" with a radical social ecology. For Bookchin "environmentalism" was merely environmental engineering based on a technocratic rationality that only suggested tinkering with existing social institutions, technologies and values. But Bookchin's alternative to "environmentalism" (or "shallow" ecology) seems to me to carry far more intellectual and political substance than the "deep ecology" suggested by Naess. The basic principles of deep ecology Naess outlines as follows:

1. That the richness and diversity of life forms have an intrinsic value in themselves and that they contribute to the flourishing of humans and non-humans alike, and that we should in no way reduce this diversity except to satisfy vital needs. At present humans are interfering in non-human life forms in an unnecessarily destructive and excessive way and this needs to be understood and curbed.

2. That the world is overpopulated with humans and that this is causing serious problems to life on earth — "life" for Naess being used in a comprehensive sense to cover not only living forms but rivers, landscapes, cultures, ecosystems, and the living earth itself.

3. That fundamental changes are necessary in basic economic, technological and ideological structures, and in individual life styles — Naess clearly addressing himself to those in Europe and North America who enjoy "high standards of living'.

Naess suggests that "economic growth" is completely incompatible with these basic principles, but it is of interest that nowhere in the book does Naess directly address himself to social problems — poverty, inequality, racism, state repression, neo-colonialism, exploitation — all of which are directly linked to environmental issues — even though his" normative" premises indicate his opposition to these. In fact, given his emphasis on ideological transformations, on self-realisation, and on individual life styles, Naess offers little in the way of exploring the underlying causes of the present ecological crisis, other than to offer a general indictment of the present economic "system'.

In outlining his philosophical worldview and in his advocacy of an "ecological consciousness" Naess has many interesting and important things to say — on the need for a "gestalt" or relational way of thinking; on the need to reflect on, and explicitly articulate the basic norms of an alternative ontology, and to avoid as far as possible purely instrumental norms; and on the problems of making ecology itself into an all-encompassing "ism," as if it were a universal science. But Naess' discussion is marred, and its flow continually disrupted, by philosophical scholasticism and at times jargon. As with the positivists the dichotomy between facts (hypotheses) and values (norms) runs like a silver thread throughout the text, although being a moral philosopher in the tradition of Spinoza, Naess, far from dismissing values, stresses their priority and importance. Yet although the idea that basic norms are not logically derived from factual hypotheses may be true, Naess" suggestion that they are therefore in some degree arbitrary verges on sophistry. Food, shelter and freedom are basic to human life, and norms related to these hypotheses are not arbitrary. Certainly humans do not live by bread alone, but only someone who does not have to worry about food and shelter, and has some degree of autonomy, could define well being in terms of such high level "ultimate goals" as pleasure, happiness and perfection.

But quite apart from the normative level on which much of Naess' discussion moves, there is also his insatiable tendency to lapse into almost impenetrable philosophical jargon. For example, while in essence properly questioning the classical Cartesian distinction between the epistemological subject and the objective world — a distinction which Hegel and many generations of philosophers and social scientists have long made redundant with their stress on the social nature of humans — Naess asks the "somewhat academic question" as to whether qualities such as hot or red or sombre adhere to the subject or to the objective world. And then to clarify this abstruse question, he writes: "A tree's sombreness is represented by the relation symbol S (A,B,C,D,...) where A could be a location on a map, B location of observer, C emotional status of person, D linguistic competence of the describer." (p65)

Even if one is interested in such epistemological problems as the relationship between subjectivism and objectivism — which presupposes the classical epistemology — one gets lost in such abstractions. But this is to make a philosophical point — one long ago made by the pragmatists, Hegelian-Marxists, and existentialists. What about his equation of what constitutes well-being?

$$W = \frac{G^2}{P_b + P_m}$$

Where W = well-being, G = glow (passion), Pb = bodily pains and Pm = mental pains (p.81). This is quantitative mysticism, expressing what to most people is fairly obvious. Even better — and even more obfuscating — is his discussion of needs.

Let A represent a living being in a time-dimensional space having four vital needs to satisfy... The quadruple a 1/1 to a 1/4 symbolises the four sources of need satisfaction... If the sources are a 2/1, a 2/3, a 2/5, a 2/7, and separated from A by interposed, qualitatively different parts a 1/1 to a 1/4 of the environment, the organism is vitally and normally dependent upon the control of these parts and also of a 2/2, a 2/4, a 2/8, the parts adjacent to the sources with another set of qualitatively different properties, (p205)

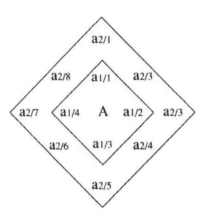

This convoluted discussion is simply — it seems — to illustrate the evident truism that "the requirement of control increases with the remoteness of sources of satisfaction of needs."

This abstract theorising does not cease when Naess in later chapters discusses technology and lifestyle, economics and ecopolitics. This is a pity given the interesting things he has to say. He stresses in Gandhian fashion the importance of linking changes in personal life style with political action, and the importance of non-violent direct action. Drawing a distinction between action, campaigns and social movements, Naess pleads for the continuation of struggles even if specific actions and campaigns appear to have been unsuccessful. But when he comes to discuss the state and the present economic system — Naess never brings himself to describe it as capitalism — Naess expresses very ambivalent attitudes. He continually emphasises, often in strident terms, that the present economic system must be fundamentally transformed. The goal of the deep ecology movement, he writes, cannot be achieved without a "deep change" of present industrial societies. Seeing contemporary environmental problems as being overcome solely by technical means reflects a "shallow" ecological approach — what is needed are fundamental changes in consciousness and the economic system. Yet he follows — and quotes approvingly — Erik Dammann's suggestion that it is far too simple to claim that capitalists, industrial magnates, bureaucrats and politicians alone have the power to preserve the system, implying that people in democratic countries (so-called) are free to make the changes if they desire. But then the disclaimer completely obscures the real causes of the environmental problems we now face — which are intrinsically related to an economic system, namely capitalism, which for centuries has been one of tyranny and exploitation, and which is based on the endless pursuit of profit. And to think that power lies in parliaments reflects a very limited conception of power under monopoly capitalism.

Drawing up a political triangle of red, blue and green, Naess sees "green" as transcending the opposition between blue (capitalism) and red (socialism). He can only do this by making some very dubious equations. The greens (deep ecology) have affinity, he suggests, with the blues in valuing personal enterprise and in opposing bureaucracies. But, of course, supporters of capitalism when they talk about freedom and personal enterprise and initiative are not really concerned with the freedom of the individual but only with the needs of private "capital." When the latter is challenged freedom goes by the board, and capitalist enterprises are highly bureaucratic. And when Naess distances himself from the reds (socialism) — which he sees as bureaucratic and as supporting industrialism and "big industry" — what he does is to equate socialism with the state capitalism of the Soviet Union, as do most apologists for capitalism.

Yet when Naess writes that the aims and values of the society cannot change unless the way of production is altered, when he speaks out for decentralisation and for the importance of social justice, and when he writes that "The utopians of green societies point towards a kind of direct democracy with local control of the means of production as the best means of achieving the goals" (p158), all he does of course is to suggest socialist ideas that communist anarchists and libertarian socialists have been propagating for a century or more. Like many in the ecology movement Naess seems quite oblivious to the libertarian socialist tradition and so offers suggestions for a "new renaissance" that are anything but new or original. He makes no reference at all to Bookchin, let alone any of the earlier anarchists.

Yet paradoxically this advocate of direct democracy and critic of contemporary capitalism makes two glaring admissions. The first is to suggest that there is hardly any capitalistic political ideology (p156). What on earth is liberalism, fascism, Thatcherism, and the so-called "enterprise culture" — not to mention intellectual fashions like socio- biology? Capitalist ideology — with its emphasis on competition, on efficiency, on management, on monitoring, on privatisation, and on so- called free enterprise — permeates current social and political thought, and libertarian and real socialist thought hardly gets a hearing in any of the major institutions and cultural arenas. Democracy ends as soon as you enter the office or factory gate. Naess" own book is infused with terms and ideas implicitly drawn from the capitalist paradigm — even when he is arguing against its tendencies. Naess makes, for instance, a very cogent critique of the "quantification" (and the attempts to put a price tag on nature) that is so dominant in shaping the policies and attitudes of contemporary societies — but it is all done very much in the language of the market economists.

Secondly, although advocating decentralisation, Naess suggests that in order to counter the increasing population pressure and war "some fairly strong central political institutions" (p157) are necessary, and to keep transnational corporations in check we may in the future have to envision global institutions with some power "not only to criticise certain states and companies but also to implement certain measures against the states which violate the rules" (p139). This is virtually the advocacy of a global state, the totalitarian implications of which are too ghastly to behold — but it is paradoxically suggested by Naess in order to safeguard "green communities" from the forces of disruption and violence.

Although Naess argues for a biocentric approach towards nature, and stresses that all life forms should be seen as having intrinsic value — the principle of "biospherical egalitarianism" — he is aware of the limitations of this principle and never lapses like other deep ecologists into misanthropy. Taken literally or seriously "biocentric equality" would of course lead to the quick demise of the human species. What however Naess suggests is that we use this principle or norm as a "guideline" — that we do not inflict unnecessary suffering upon other living beings, and that we treat all aspects of nature as having intrinsic value. He is aware that human praxis and the human condition necessarily involves a transgression of this norm, and that some killing and exploitation of non-human life forms is unavoidable. But his point is that this instrumentality should be kept to a minimum, and only serve vital human needs — for sustenance and shelter. Unlike many other ecologists — and many vegetarians — he is aware that among many tribal communities a sense of kinship or identification with nature coexists with a hunting culture. Unlike other ecologists too, Naess doesn't deny the importance of humans, or treat humankind as if it were a blot upon the landscape. Like Bookchin he recognises that there is a certain uniqueness about humans on earth — but he strongly argues that this uniqueness must not be used as a premise for the domination of nature, and for treating other life-forms simply as a means to human satisfaction. But rather it must be used as a premise for a universal care that other species can neither understand nor afford (p171). And this concern extends to humans, for social justice is an important component of his philosophy — "no exploitation," "no subjection" and "no class societies" are constituent norms of his rather abstract normative schema.

The most fundamental norm for Naess and the logical starting point of his whole philosophy is the idea of Self-realisation — the self having a capital S. All other norms are derived from this key idea. But he is ambivalent about what this Self stands for. He writes that this Self is known throughout the history of philosophy under such names as "the Universal Self, "the Absolute," "the atman." But in the religious traditions from which these terms derive Self does not imply an identification with nature but rather has spiritual connotations, and the discovery of the Self means the identification with god, the absolute or Brahman. For example, atman means that spiritual aspect of the person (soul) which is distinct from the mind, sense organs and the physical body, and self realisation (moksha, or salvation) entails the realisation that this soul is in fact Brahman — the supreme Self or world spirit. In this Vedanta tradition the natural world is an illusion (maya). In other religious traditions, as Naess himself writes, the spirit (soul) was considered radically distinct from the body, and the body and the material world were seen as a positive hindrance to self-realisation. In the gnostic tradition the body is seen as a temporary "prison" or "tomb" of the soul (self) and, as Hans Jonas has perceptively written, this radical religious dualism — exemplified in the European tradition by Platonism, gnosticism and Judeo-Christianity — is an essential precursor of mechanistic philosophy and anthropocentrism.[6] This form of religious Self realisation is profoundly anti-ecological — for as Naess suggests in writing about Plotinus, it involves a "depreciation of physical reality." As he writes "A search for supernatural being can easily become an endeavour hostile to man and environment" (p190) — but of course this is precisely what most mystical traditions entail — the detachment of self from organic life. What Naess seems to be suggesting however is something quite different: for the "oneness" he suggests is not the identification of the self with god, the absolute or world spirit (Brahman), but rather the identification of the person with the natural world (in his case, especially with mountains). And in this, of course, he follows Spinoza and such nature mystics as Richard Jefferies. Although he seems to suggest that Spinoza was influenced by the idea of an "immanent God" (p201), Spinoza's philosophy was in fact something quite different, for he equated

God with nature, and advocated a religious atheism or a profane mysticism. He advocated a salvation ethic in which god is neither a transcendental nor immanent spirit but nature itself. Naess seems to suggest a similar ethic — a "philosophy of oneness" — in which a deep identification with the natural world is felt or experienced. It is an "ecological consciousness," or the development of an "ecological self that goes beyond the narrow ego and the ordinary self (with a small "s"). Naess thus seems to play down the "spiritual" interpretation — God is hardly mentioned — and is sceptical of a mystical oneness. What we have to do, he writes, is to walk a difficult ridge: "To the left we have the ocean of organic and mystic views, to the right the abyss of atomic individualism" (p165).

Naess writes as a philosopher rather than as a social theorist, and although he stresses the importance of community, autonomy, local self-sufficiency and co-operation, and decentralisation, the discussion of these always tends to be rather abstract — "normative." There is therefore very little in the book about bioregionalism, about feminism, about neighbourhood associations, or about the communitarian movements and anarchist collectives that have been erupting throughout history to challenge capitalist exploitation and hierarchy. And the stress he puts on changing one's life style and on "self-realisation" while perhaps important to the white affluent middle classes of Europe and North America, can all too easily lead to a politics of "survivalism." Following Gandhi, Naess stresses the importance of political action, but such action as he envisages tends to focus on "symptoms" — on environmental issues — rather than directly challenging the primary social institutions of the capitalist system — the multinational corporations and state structures that support them. Indeed in the future ecological society that he postulates after the radical transformation of the present system, he seems to envisage the continued existence of both these capitalist firms and the nation state — so one wonders how radical or "deep" is the transformation that Naess envisages?

DEEP ECOLOGY, ANARCHO—SYNDICALISM AND THE FUTURE OF ANARCHIST THOUGHT
by Murray Bookchin

There is very little I can add to the outstanding criticism Brian Morris levels at deep ecology. Indeed, Morris's contribution to the debate around eco-mysticism generally has been insightful as well as incisive, and I have found his writings an educational experience that hopefully will reach a very wide audience in the United States in addition to Britain.

I should hope that his review of Arne Naess's *Ecology, Community and Lifestyle* has revealed the intellectual poverty of the "father of deep ecology" and the silliness of the entire deep ecology "movement." Rodney Aitchtey's rather airy, often inaccurate, and mystical *Deep Ecology: Not Man Apart*, it would seem to me, is perhaps the best argument against deep ecology that I have seen in quite a while. But after dealing with deep ecologists in North America for quite a few years, I have reluctantly come to the conclusion that the acolytes of Naess et al operate on faith and are motivated in their allegiances by theological rather than rational impulses. There is no reasoned argument, I suspect, that will shake a belief-system of this kind — hence I will leave discussion of the issues involved to others who still have the energy to deal with mindless dogmas.

I would add — or possibly reinforce — only one observation to the incisive ones that Morris makes. One wonders whether deep ecology's biocentric maxim that all living beings can be equatable with one another in terms of their "intrinsic worth" would have had any meaning during the long eras of organic evolution before human beings emerged. The entire conceptual framework of deep ecology is entirely a product of human agency — a fact that imparts to the human species a unique status in the natural world. All ethical systems (including those that can be grounded in biotic evolution) are formulated by human beings in distinctly cultural situations. Remove human agency from the scene, and there is not the least evidence that animals exhibit behaviour that can be regarded as discursive, meaningful, or moral. When Elisée Reclus, the anarchist geographer, tells us that pussycats are (as cited by George Woodcock in his introduction to the Marie Fleming biography of Reclus) "natural anarchists," or worse, that "there is not a human sentiment which on occasion they [i.e. cats] do not understand or share, not an idea which they do not divine [sic!], not a desire but what they forestall it," Reclus is writing ethological and ecological nonsense.

That anarchist writers celebrate the author of such an anthropomorphic absurdity as "ecological" is regrettable to say the least. To the extent that "intrinsic worth" is something more than merely an agreeable intuition in modern ecological thought, it is an "attribute" that human beings formulate in their minds and a "right" that they may decide to confer on animals and other creatures. It does not exist apart from the operations of the human mind or humanity's social values.

To turn from the silliness of deep ecology to the preposterous elucidation of anarcho-syndicalism that Graham Purchase advances is a thankless task that I would ignore were it not scheduled to be published in book form. Purchase's piece, *Social Ecology, Anarchism and Trade Unionism*, is a malicious essay that begins by accusing me of writing belligerently and "insult(ing) American anarchists and trade unionists," then goes on to heap upon me some of the most vituperative and ad hominem attacks that I've encountered in a long time. Not only am I "at best unconstructive and at worst positively harmful," Purchase warns his readers, but worse, I am consumed by "an insatiable appetite for controversy."

Having advanced this no doubt balanced, unprovocative, and objective evaluation of my role in the anarchist movement, Purchase displays his psychoanalytic acumen by alleging that I suffer from "an unhealthy desire to be the intellectual leader and founder of a "new" ecological movement," that I exhibit evidence of "intellectual schizophrenia," and finally that I "filch all the major ecological insights of anarchist theory and practice [and] dress them up in a socialist-feminist [!] cum neo-Hegelian garb and go on to more or less claim them as [my] own." As if this level of vituperation were not enough — no doubt it is intended to subdue my own "insatiable appetite for controversy!" — Purchase goes on to characterize the body of views that I have advanced over a dozen or so books and scores of articles as "an intellectual outrage'.

To correct Purchase's often convoluted account of the evolution of my views — presumably I was an "anarchist-ecologist" in the late 1960s and '70s, only to mutate into an "outrageous" anti-syndicalist and hence anti-anarchist "social ecologist" in the 1980s and '90s — would be as tedious as it would be futile. I shall leave it to serious readers of my work to sort out the absurdities of his account. Suffice it here to make a few points. No-one, least of all I, believes that we can radically alter society without the support of the proletariat and working people of all kinds. But to assume that industrial workers will play the "hegemonic" role that Marxists traditionally assigned to them — and that the anarcho-syndicalists merely echoed — is to smother radical thought and practice with a vengeance.

My criticism of theories that assign a hegemonic role to the proletariat in the struggle for an anarchist society — generically denoted by labour historians as "proletarian socialism" — is simply that they are obsolete. The reasons for the passage of the era of proletarian socialism into history have been explored not only by myself but by serious radical theorists of all kinds — including anarchists. From decades of experience in my own life, I learned that industrial workers can more easily be reached as men and women, husbands and wives, fathers and mothers, brothers and sisters, indeed, as neighbours and citizens. They are often more concerned about community problems, pollution, public education, democracy, morality, and the quality of their lives than about whether they "control" the factories in which they are ruthlessly exploited. Indeed, the majority of workers and trade-union members with whom I worked for years in foundries and auto plants were more eager to get out of their factories after working hours were over than to ponder production schedules and vocational assignments.

Is it inconceivable that we have misread the historical nature of the proletariat (more a Marxian failing, I may add, than a traditional anarchist one) as a revolutionary hegemonic class? Is it inconceivable that the factory system, far from organising and radicalising the proletariat, has steadily assimilated it to industrial systems of command and obedience? Have capitalism and the working class stood still since the nineteenth and early 20th centuries, or have they both undergone profound changes that pose major challenges to — and significantly vitiate the claims of — anarcho-syndicalists as well as traditional Marxists? With remarkable prescience, Bakunin himself expressed his fears about the possible "embourgeoisement" of the working class and, more generally, that the "masses have allowed themselves to become deeply demoralized, apathetic, not to say castrated by the pernicious influence of our corrupt, centralised, Statist civilisation." Bakunin's fears were not merely an expression of a strategic view that applies only to his own time, but a historic judgment that still requires explication, not equivocation. Today, so-called "progressive" capitalist enterprises have succeeded quite admirably by giving workers an appreciable share in hiring, firing and setting production quotas, bringing the proletariat into complicity with its own exploitation.

Purchase not only ignores these momentous developments and the analyses that I and others have advanced; he grossly misinterprets and demagogically redefines any criticism of syndicalism, indeed, trade-unionism, as an expression of hostility toward anarchism as such. Assuming that Purchase knows very much about the history of anarchism and syndicalism, this line of argument is manipulative and an outright distortion; but to be generous, I will say that it reveals a degree of ignorance and intolerance that deserves vigorous reproval. In fact, in the late nineteenth century, when syndicalism emerged as an issue among anarchists, it was furiously debated. The outstanding luminaries of the anarchist movement at the turn of the century — such as Errico Malatesta, Elisée Reclus, Emma Goldman, Sebastian Faure, and others — initially opposed syndicalism for a variety of reasons, many of which show a great deal of prescience on their part. And in time, when they came to accept it, many of them did so in a highly prudent manner. Malatesta, in his fundamental criticism of syndicalism, argued that the generation of a revolutionary spirit "cannot be the normal, natural definition of the trade union's function." Although he eventually accepted anarcho-syndicalism with apparent reluctance, he continued to call for a far more expansive form of anarchist organisation and practice than many syndicalists were prepared to accept.

In practice, anarchist groups often came into outright conflict with anarcho-syndicalist organisations — not to speak of syndicalist organisations, many of which eschewed anarchism. Early in the century, the Spanish anarcho-communists, influenced primarily by Juan Baron and Francisco Cardinal, the editors of *Tierra y Libertad*, furiously denounced the anarcho-syndicalists who were later to form the CNT as "deserters" and "reformists." Similar conflicts developed in Italy, France, and the United States, and perhaps not without reason. The record of the anarcho-syndicalist movement has been one of the most abysmal in the history of anarchism generally. In the Mexican Revolution, for example, the anarcho-syndicalist leaders of the Casa del Obrero Mundial shamefully placed their proletarian "Red Battalions" at the service of Carranza, one of the revolution's most bloodthirsty thugs, to fight the truly revolutionary militia of Zapata — all to gain a few paltry reforms, which Carranza withdrew once the Zapatista challenge had been broken with their collaboration. The great Mexican anarchist Ricardo Flores Magón justly denounced their behaviour as a betrayal.

Nor can much be said in defence of the leaders of the CNT in Spain. They swallowed their libertarian principles by becoming "ministers" in the Madrid government late in 1936, not without the support of many of their followers, I should add, and in May 1937 they used their prestige to disarm the Barcelona proletariat when it tried to resist the Stalinist counterrevolution in the Catalan capital. In the United States, lest present-day anarcho-syndicalists get carried away by legendary movements like the Industrial Workers of the World (IWW), they should be advised that this syndicalist movement, like others elsewhere, was by no means committed to anarchism. "Big Bill" Haywood, its most renowned leader, was never an anarchist.

Still other IWW leaders, many of whom tilted toward an anarchist outlook, not only became Communists in the 1920s but became ardent Stalinists in the '30s and later. It is worth noting that serious Spanish anarchists, even those who joined the CNT, regarded the influence of the CNT's trade-unionist mentality on the FAI (Iberian Anarchist Federation) as deleterious and ultimately disastrous. Toward the end of the civil war, it was questionable whether the FAI controlled the CNT or, more likely, whether the CNT, with its strong trade-union mentality, had essentially diluted the FAI's anarchist principles. As Malatesta had so perceptively declared, even as he cautiously accepted the amalgamation of anarchist with syndicalist principles under the pressure of a growing syndicalist movement in Europe, "trade unions are, by their nature, reformist and never revolutionary" (emphasis added). For an oaf like Graham Purchase to bombastically equate syndicalism with anarchism — an act of arrogance that is as fatuous as it is ignorant — and then to go on and essentially equate trade unionism with syndicalism deserves only disdain.

The authentic locus of anarchists in the past was the commune or municipality, not the factory, which was generally conceived as only part of a broader communal structure, not its decisive component. Syndicalism, to the extent that it narrowed this broader outlook by singling out the proletariat and its industrial environment as its locus, also crucially narrowed the more sweeping social and moral landscape that traditional anarchism had created. In large part, this ideological retreat reflected the rise of the factory system in the closing years of the last century in France and Spain, but it also echoed the ascendancy of a particularly vulgar form of economistic Marxism (Marx, to his credit, did not place much stock in trade unionism), to which many naive anarchists and nonpolitical trade unionists succumbed. *After the Revolution* by Abad de Santillan, one of the movers and shakers of Spanish anarcho-syndicalism, reflects this shift toward a pragmatic economism in such a way that makes his views almost indistinguishable from those of the Spanish socialists — and, of course, that brought him into collusion with the Catalan government, literally one of the grave-diggers of Spanish anarchism. Syndicalism — be it anarcho-syndicalism or its less libertarian variants — has probably done more to denature the ethical content of anarchism than any other single factor in the history of the movement, apart from anarchism's largely marginal and ineffectual individualist tendencies. Indeed, until anarchism shakes off this syndicalist heritage and expands its communalistic and communistic heritage, it will be little more than a rhetorical and mindless echo of vulgar Marxism and the ghost of an era that has long passed into history.

But as the Germans say, genug! I've had it with Purchase and his kind. Let them explore more thoroughly the historical and textual bases of anarchist theory and practice before they leap into print with inanities that reveal their appalling ignorance of the intellectual and practical trajectories of their own beliefs. And they should also take some pains to read what I have written on the history and failings of the workers" movement before they undertake to criticize my own views. What I strongly resent, however, is the fatuous implication — one that even more sensible anarchists sometimes imply — that I "filch" my ecological views from" anarchist theory and practice." In fact, I have been overly eager to cite anarchist antecedents for social ecology (as I call my eco-anarchist views), and I have done so wherever I could. *The Ecology of Freedom*, written in 1982 — that is, during the period when, according to Purchase, I abandoned my anarchist views for social ecology — opens with an epigraph from Kropotkin's *Ethics*. In the Acknowledgments section of that book, I observed that "Peter Kropotkin's writings on mutual aid and anarchism remain an abiding tradition to which I am committed." For reasons that I shall explain, this is a bit of an overstatement so far as Kropotkin is concerned, but the text contains no less than nine favourable, often laudatory references to him, including an extensive quotation from *Mutual Aid* with which I expressed my warm approval. If I have not mentioned Elisée Reclus, it was because I knew nothing about his work and views until I read Marie Fleming's 1988 biography of him for the first time only a few weeks ago. And in retrospect, I doubt that I would have quoted or cited him in any case.

Try as I have to cite my affinity with anarchist writers of the past, guardians of the anarchist ossuary often miss a very crucial point. Social ecology is a fairly integrated and coherent viewpoint that encompasses a philosophy of natural evolution and of humanity's place in that evolutionary process; a reformulation of dialectics along ecological lines; an account of the emergence of hierarchy; a historical examination of the dialectic between legacies and epistemologies of domination and freedom; an evaluation of technology from an historical, ethical, and philosophical standpoint; a wide-ranging critique of Marxism, the Frankfurt School, justice, rationalism, scientism, and instrumentalism; and finally, an eduction of a vision of a utopian, decentralized, confederal, and aesthetically grounded future society based on an objective ethics of complementarity. I do not present these ideas as a mere inventory of subjects but as a highly coherent viewpoint. *The Ecology of Freedom*, moreover, must be supplemented by the later *Urbanization Without Cities*, *The Philosophy of Social Ecology*, and *Remaking Society*, not to speak of quite a few important essays published mainly in *Green Perspectives*, if one is to recognise that social ecology is more than the sum of its parts.

Whether adequately or not, the holistic body of ideas in these works endeavours to place "eco-anarchism," a term that to the best of my knowledge has come into existence entirely as a result of my writings, on a theoretical and intellectual par with the best systematic works in radical social theory. To pick this corpus apart by citing an antecedent, in the writings of some prominent nineteenth-century anarchists, for an idea that I developed in this whole, and thereby deal with only part of what I have tried to integrate into a meaningful and relevant whole for our times, is simply fatuous. One could similarly reduce systematic accounts of any body of social or even scientific theory by citing historical antecedents for various constituent fragments. If there is any "filching" going on, it may well be by the guardians of the anarchist ossuary who have turned the rather smug boast "We said it long ago" into a veritable industry, while themselves benefiting from whatever prestige anarchism has gained over the past decades by virtue of its association with social ecology.

I would not make such an assertion, had I not been provoked by the arrogance and dogmatism of these guardians in my encounters with them. To set the record straight: The fact is that Kropotkin had no influence on my turn from Marxism to anarchism — nor, for that matter, did Bakunin or Proudhon. It was Herbert Read's *The Philosophy of Anarchism* that I found most useful for rooting the views that I slowly developed over the fifties and well into the '60s in a libertarian pedigree; hence the considerable attention he received in my 1964 essay, *Ecology and Revolutionary Thought*. Odd as it may seem, it was my reaction against Marx and Engels's critiques of anarchism, my readings into the Athenian polis, George Woodcock's informative history of anarchism, my own avocation as a biologist, and my studies in technology that gave rise to the views in my early essays — not any extensive readings into the works of early anarchists. Had I been "born into" the anarchist tradition, as some of our more self-righteous anarchists claim to have been, I might well have taken umbrage at Proudhon's exchange-oriented contractualism, and after my long experience in the workers" movement, I would have felt smothered by the rubbish about syndicalism advanced by Graham Purchase and his kind.

Purchase's fatuous attempt to distinguish my post-1980 writings on social ecology from my presumably "true-blue" anarchist writings before that date leaves a number of facts about the development of social ecology unexplained. I wrote my earliest, almost book-length work on the ecological dislocations produced by capitalism, "The Problems of Chemicals in Food," in 1952, while I was a neo-Marxist and had in no way been influenced by anarchist thinkers. Many of Marx's views heavily contributed to my notion of post-scarcity, very much a "pre-1980" outlook to which I still adhere. (Certain Spanish anarchists, I may add, held similar views in the 1930s, as I discovered decades later when I wrote The Spanish anarchists.) I say all of this without being in the least concerned that my anarchist views may be "adulterated" by some of Marx's concepts.

With Bakunin, I share the view that Marx made invaluable contributions to radical theory, contributions one can easily value without accepting his authoritarian politics or perspectives. For anarchists to foolishly demonise Marx — or even Hegel, for that matter — is to abandon a rich legacy of ideas that should be brought to the service of libertarian thought, just as the fascinating work of many biologists should be brought to the service of ecological thought. Which does not mean that we have to accept Marx's gross errors about centralism, his commitment to a "worker's party," his support of the nation-state, and the like, any more than learning from Hegel's dialectic means that we must necessarily accept the existence of an "absolute," a strict teleological system, a hybridised corporate-parliamentary monarchy, or what he broadly called "absolute idealism."

By the same token, we will be deceiving nobody but ourselves if we celebrate the insights of traditional anarchism without dealing forthrightly with its shortcomings. Due honour should certainly be given to Proudhon for developing federalistic notions of social organisation against the nation-state and defending the rights of craftspeople and peasants who were under the assault of industrial capitalism — a system that Marx dogmatically celebrated in so many of his writings.

But it would be sheer myopia to ignore Proudhon's commitment to a contractual form of economic relationships, as distinguished from the communistic maxim "From each according to his or her abilities, to each according to his or her needs." His contractualism permeated his federalistic concepts and can scarcely be distinguished from bourgeois conceptions of "right." I say this despite some attempts that have been made to cast his proclivity for contractual exchanges into a quasi-philosophical notion of "social contract." Even if Proudhonism really were a social contract theory, this would be quite unsatisfactory, in my eyes.

Nor can we ignore Richard Vernon's observation in his introduction to Proudhon's *The Principle of Federalism* that Proudhon viewed federalism as an abridgment of his earlier, largely personalistic anarchism. If thought out carefully, Proudhon's views seem to be premised on the existence of free-floating, seemingly "sovereign" individuals, craftspersons, or even collectives structured around contractual, exchange like relationships and property ownership rather than on a communistic system of "ownership" and distribution of goods.

Bakunin, in turn, was an avowed collectivist, not a communist, and his views on organisation in particular were often at odds with themselves. (I might remind Purchase, here, that Fourier was in no sense a socialist, anarchist or even a revolutionary, despite his many rich insights.) Maximoff's later assemblage of small portions of Bakunin's many writings under the rubric of "scientific anarchism" would probably have astonished Bakunin, just as many of Bakunin's insights would shock orthodox anarchists today. I, for one, would generally agree with Bakunin, for example, that "municipal elections always best reflect the real attitude and will of the people," although I would want to restate his formulation to mean that municipal elections can more accurately reflect the popular will than parliamentary ones. But how many orthodox anarchists would agree with Bakunin's view — or even my qualified one? The extreme resistance I have encountered from anarchist traditionalists and "purists" on this issue has virtually foreclosed any possibility of developing a libertarian, participatory, municipalist, and confederal politics today as part of the anarchist tradition.

Given his time and place, Kropotkin was perhaps one of the most far-seeing of the theorists I encountered in the libertarian tradition. It was not until the late '60s, when reprints of his works began to appear in American bookshops, that I became familiar with his *Fields, Factories, and Workshops* (and at a later time, Colin Ward's excellent abridgment of this book), and it was not until the mid-'60s that I read portions of *Mutual Aid* — that is, the centre portion that deals with medieval cities. To be quite frank, these books did not appreciably affect my views; rather, they confirmed them and reinforced my commitment to anarchism.

In much the same way, my 1974 book *The Limits of the City*, structured around a very large essay I wrote in 1958, unknowingly paralleled some of Marx's observations on the relationship between town and country that he expressed in the *Grundrisse*, which was not available to me in English translation until the 1960s. Indeed, it was mainly my study of urban development over the course of history that nourished *The Limits of the City*, a work strongly influenced by Marx's *Capital*. My book mentions Kropotkin only incidentally as figuring in the history of city planning in the later-appended pages. I cite this background to note how nonsensical Purchase's distinction between my pre-1980 and my post-1980 development really is, and to point out how little Purchase seems to know about my writings, much less their "pedigree" and the diversity of ideological, philosophical, and historical sources that have nourished my writings.

Far from pillaging from Kropotkin and other anarchist writers, I have tended in the past, let me repeat, to overstate my obligation to them. I never agreed with free-booting notions of anarchism that rest as much on ordinary professional and scientific associations as they do on the broader notion of a commune based on civic unity and popular assemblies. Moreover, a revolutionism that is primarily rooted in a "revolutionary instinct" (Bakunin) and a mutualism that is primarily rooted in a "social instinct" (Kropotkin) are little more than vague substitutes for serious explanations. Instinct theory has to be dealt with very cautiously, lest it devolve into outright sociobiology. Kropotkin's rather loose attribution of "social instinct" to animals generally in order to validate mutualism is particularly troubling, in my view, not only because it is based on a highly selective study of animals — he tends to ignore a host of solitary animals, including highly advanced mammals. Even more troubling is that he tends to confuse animal troops, herds, packs, and transient communities with societies: that is to say, with highly mutable institutions, alterable as they are by virtue of the distinctly human ability to form, develop, subvert, and overthrow them according to their interests and will.

Elisée Reclus, for his part, carried certain elements of Kropotkin's outlook to the point of absurdity. I am at a loss to understand how cats "understand or share" or "forestall" our "sentiments," "desires," and "ideas," as Reclus asserted they do in the quotation I cited near the beginning of this article. I am certain that my doubts about so saintly and gentle an anarchist as Reclus will place me in the bad graces of cat owners, but I find such anthropomorphism naive. His view that "secret harmony exists between the earth and people," one that "imprudent societies" will always regret if they violate it, is far too vague, at times even mystical, to be regarded as more than a generous sentiment. One may surely respect such sentiments, but countless writers (including some very reactionary nature romantics) have reiterated them more emphatically to regard them as eco-anarchist in nature. Deep ecology, eco-theology, and air-headed spiritualists have found more "secret harmonies" between humanity and nonhuman nature than I know what to do with. I would certainly praise Reclus as an anarchist and a resolute revolutionary, but I would be disquieted if his particular views on the natural world were identified, apart from their good intentions, with eco-anarchism.

Yes, let us give Proudhon, Bakunin, Kropotkin, Reclus, Malatesta, and other leading anarchist thinkers due honour and respect for what they did in their time and what they have to offer to ours. But cannot anarchism go further than the terrain they charted out a century ago? If some of us try to do so, must we live under the tyranny of ossuary guardians like Graham Purchase, who can be expected to lift a bony finger from out of the crypt and reprove us for ignoring 19th-century anarchists" passages on ecologically oriented social relationships and humanity's relationship to nature — a hint here, an antecedent fragment there, even a sizeable passage — whose formulations are inadequate today and were often quite erroneous to begin with? We can certainly build on views advanced by the great anarchist thinkers of the past. But must we ignore the need for more sophisticated notions of confederalism, anti-Statism, decentralism, definitions of freedom, and sensitivity to the natural world, than those that they advanced? There are many notions that were central to their views that we are obliged to discard. Such advances, hopefully, and the coherence they provide are part of the history of cultural development as a whole. Is anarchism to be immunised from further developments and revisions by the guardians of its ossuary? I would hope not, especially since anarchism — almost by definition — is the exercise of freedom not only in the social realm but also in the realm of thought. To lock anarchism into a crypt and condemn any innovative body of libertarian ideas as booty "filched" from a sacred precinct is an affront to the libertarian spirit and all that the libertarian tradition stands for.

Times do change. The proletariat and, more marginally, the peasantry to which anarcho-syndicalism turned as a "historical subject," or agents for revolution, are numerically diminishing at best or are being integrated into the existing system at worst. The most crucial contradictions of capitalism are not those within the system but between the system and the natural world. Today, a broad consensus is growing among all oppressed people — by no means strictly industrial workers — that ecological dislocation has produced monumental problems, problems that may well bring the biosphere as we know it to an end. With the emergence of a general human interest, largely the need to maintain and restore a viable biosphere, an interest around which people of highly disparate backgrounds and social strata may yet unite, anarcho-syndicalism is simply archaic, both as a movement and as a body of ideas. If anarchist theory and practice cannot keep pace with — let alone go beyond — historic changes that have altered the entire social, cultural, and moral landscape and effaced a good part of the world in which traditional anarchism was developed, the entire movement will indeed become what Theodor Adorno called it — "a ghost." If every attempt to provide a coherent, contemporary interpretation of the anarchist tradition is fragmented, shattered, and parcelled out to antecedents whose views were often more appropriate to their times than they are to ours, the libertarian tradition will fade back into history as surely as the anarchic anabaptists have disappeared. Then capitalism and the Right will indeed have society completely under their control, and self-styled libertarian ideas may well become relics in an ideological museum that will be as remote to the coming century as Jacobinism is to our own.

July 11th, 1992

MURRAY BOOKCHIN'S LEGACY
by Brian Morris

Although Murray Bookchin has been described as one of the most provocative, exciting and original political thinkers of the 20th century it is noteworthy that he is singularly ignored by many academic scholars working in green philosophy or on the history of the ecology movement, while he is invariably caricatured or reduced to a negative stereotype by anarcho-primitivists and spiritual ecologists.

In this essay I am aiming to outline and reaffirm Bookchin's enduring legacy as an important scholar, both in terms of his philosophy of nature — dialectical or evolutionary naturalism, and in terms of his radical politics — libertarian socialism or communalism. For Bookchin's political legacy offers the only real solution to the immense social and ecological problems that now confront us, as neither communing with the spirit world (spiritualism) nor the technocratic solutions offered within the current capitalist system will suffice.

In a recent critically-acclaimed text *Facing the Anthropocene* Ian Angus writes, with respect to the present crisis of the Earth system, specifically global warming, that it is "a challenge to everyone who cares about humanity's future to face up to the fact that survival in the Anthropocene requires radical social change, replacing fossil capitalism with an ecological civilisation, eco-socialism. He neglects to mention, of course, that this is something that Murray Bookchin was extolling over 40 years ago, although, for Bookchin, this did not entail that "we need governments" in order to create an ecological society. For Bookchin, following Bakunin and Kropotkin, always felt that Marxist politics, specifically the "conquest" of State power, would lead only to either reformism, or, as in Russia and China, to State capitalism and political tyranny.

Both a radical activist and an important radical scholar, for over 50 years Murray Bookchin (1921-2006) produced a steady stream of essays, political tracts and substantial books on environmental issues, on the culture of cities, on libertarian political movements, and on social ecology that are truly impressive and path-breaking. Yet he remained one of the key figures in the ecology movement not to succumb either to religious mysticism or to fashionable postmodernism, but stayed true to the rationalist tradition of the radical Enlightenment.

Throughout his life he was an evolutionary naturalist, as well as a libertarian socialist — a leftist and a revolutionary.

The notion that in his later years Bookchin became a "grumpy old man," that he abandoned his earlier ecological vision and attempted to "trash" his own political legacy seems to me highly misleading. Granted that, given his polemical writings, Bookchin came to be assailed on all sides — by deep ecologists, political liberals, technophobes, anarcho-primitivists, spiritualist ecologists, neo-Marxists and Stirnerite egoists, as well as by the acolytes of Nietzsche and Heidegger. In many ways he became an isolated figure. Yet in an important sense, Murray Bookchin remained throughout his life a committed and passionate evolutionary naturalist and a revolutionary anarchist — that is, a libertarian socialist.

The situationists mockingly described Bookchin as "Smokey the Bear." In many ways this is a fitting description, for he was gruff, solid, down to earth and enraged at the state of the world and committed to doing something about it. Bookchin was a coherent thinker and all aspects of his work are closely inter-related. I shall focus in this essay on some of his key ideas, and will outline this legacy in terms of four themes — which I discuss in turn. Namely the modern crisis, social ecology, dialectical naturalism and ethics, and finally Bookchin's libertarian socialism.

The Modern Crisis

Along with Rachel Carson, Barry Commoner and Rene Dubos, Bookchin was one of the key figures in the rise of the ecology movement around 1970s. There is no doubt that when I first became involved in environmental issues in the 1960s ecology was very much seen as a radical movement. Indeed biologist Paul Sears had described ecology as the "subversive science."

The writings of Bookchin, as well as those of the Marxist Barry Commoner emphasised that we were confronting a severe ecological crisis that was unprecedented in human history, and that the roots of this crisis lay primarily with an economic system — capitalism — that was geared not to human wellbeing but to the generation of profit, that saw no limit to industrial progress, no limit to economic growth and technology.

Ultimately, it was felt by Bookchin that capitalism was destructive not only to ourselves, but to the whole fabric of life on Earth. For the underlying ethic of capitalism was indeed the technological domination of nature, an anthropocentric ethic that viewed a biosphere as having no intrinsic value: it was simply a resource to be exploited by capital. In his pioneering ecological study *Our Synthetic Environment* and in his various other writings Bookchin graphically outlined the social and ecological crisis that had emerged since the expansion of global capitalism at the end of the second world war.

Apart from die-hard neoconservatives, most people now recognise that the world is in a sorry state and that there is a lot to be angry about. Long ago Bookchin outlined what he described as the "modern crisis," highlighting that both global capitalism and the modern liberal State are in severe crisis. This crisis, for Bookchin, was indeed manifold: at once social, economic, political and ecological.

For under global capitalism there had been a growing concentration of economic power, and the now continuous expansion of economic inequalities. It is now estimated that the 400 richest people in the world have a combined wealth greater than that of 45% of the world's population. No wonder rampant poverty exists throughout the world. Out of a world population of seven billion people nearly one billion (an estimated 15%) are severely undernourished, that is unable to obtain the basic conditions of human existence. Such poverty is not integral to the human condition, but, as Bookchin emphasised, is directly related to "development;" that is to global expansion of capitalism.

Equally significant is that throughout the world we find a "dialectic of violence" — reflected in the widespread existence and stockpiling of weapons of mass destruction, both chemical and nuclear.

This can hardly be said to have kept the peace, for since the second world as there have been over 100 major armed conflicts, killing millions of people. This dialectic of violence has led to a disintegration of local communities, the denial of human rights, widespread genocide and political oppression, usually by governments. Not only Bookchin but many scholars have emphasised that the impact of free-market capitalism has been socially devastating, not only leading to economic inequalities and widespread poverty, but also to social chaos, political instability, ethnic conflict and family and community breakdown.

Finally, there is an "ecological" crisis — the severe ecological challenges that humans now face. As Bookchin outlined, this is clearly manifested in the degradation of the natural environment under industrial capitalism — the pollution of the atmosphere, and of the seas, lakes and rivers; widespread deforestation; the impact of industrial agriculture which, as Bookchin put it, is "simplifying" the landscape, while giving rise to the adverse effects of toxic pesticides and soil erosion; the creation of toxic wastelands, the loss of biodiversity with many species now facing extinction, the problem of chemical additives in food; and, finally, a serious decline in the quality of urban life through overcrowding, poverty and traffic congestion.

Equally important for Bookchin was that capitalism had ceased to be simply an economic system, for the market economy had come to "penetrate" (as he described it) every aspect of social life and culture. Wealthy celebrities are now extolled while greed and self-aggrandisement has come to be considered virtuous.

For Bookchin of course it was not simply that there were too many people on Earth, nor technology itself, or the mechanistic worldview of Rene Descartes that had brought upon us the "modern crisis" and the degradation of the natural environment, but rather the roots of the ecological crisis lay firmly with global capitalism that was continually "plundering the earth" in the search for profits. Bookchin indeed felt that the capitalist market economy had become a "terrifying menace" to the very integrity of life on Earth. Industrial capitalism, he argued, was fundamentally anti-ecological, and over 40 years ago Bookchin was highlighting, with some prescience, long before Al Gore, George Monbiot et al, the problem of global warming, that the burning of fossil fuels (specifically coal and oil) had created a "blanket of carbon dioxide" that would lead to destructive storm problems and eventually a melting of the ice caps and rising sea levels.

It's important to emphasise that although Bookchin recognised that humans had often damaged the natural environment in which they lived, in the past this had been essentially a local phenomenon and a local problem. But, he argued, since around 1950, with the expansion of global capitalism, humanity had come to place severe ecological burdens upon planet Earth, that were global in extent, and that have "no precedent in human history."

Two issues particularly troubled Bookchin; the possibility of a worldwide thermonuclear war, given the "balance of terror" strategies of Russia and the US, and the climatic changes that had been induced by the widespread burning of fossil fuels. Both, he felt, could have a catastrophic negative impact upon organic life, the biosphere.

What concerned Bookchin, therefore, was both "our destiny as a lifeform and the future of the biosphere itself." Contrary to the opinions of his critics — both the neo-primitivists and the mystical (deep) ecologists — Bookchin was concerned not only with the survival and wellbeing of the human species, but also with the flourishing of other lifeforms and of the Earth itself. We need, he argued, to maintain the "restorative powers" of both nature and humanity, and to "reclaim the planet for life and fecundity."

In response to the "modern crisis," especially with respect to the social and ecological challenges it invoked, Bookchin proposed a re-affirmation and a creative development of the revolutionary anarchist tradition that essentially stemmed from Michael Bakunin, Peter Kropotkin and their associates. This tradition emphasised the need to integrate an ecological worldview; a social ecology that Bookchin would later describe as "dialectical naturalism" with the political philosophy offered by anarchism, that is, libertarian socialism.

Ever since I read *Post-Scarcity Anarchism* some four decades ago I have been a fan of Bookchin, in the same way as I have been a fan of Kropotkin, Lewis Mumford, Richard Jefferies and Ernest Thompson. All were pioneer social ecologists. For in his early writing Bookchin argued that human social life and nature must be grasped in a new unity, that the time had come to integrate an ecological natural philosophy (social ecology) with a social philosophy based on freedom and mutual aid (libertarian socialism). This unity was necessary, he argued, if we were to avoid an ecological catastrophe. What we must therefore do, Bookchin stressed, was to "decentralise, restore bioregional forms of production and food cultivation, scale them to human dimensions, and establish face-to-face forms of democracy" as well as to foster a "new sensibility towards the biosphere."

Although in later years Bookchin became embroiled in rather acrimonious debates with deep ecologists, anarcho-primitivists and bourgeois individualists — in which he fervently defended his own brand of social ecology and libertarian socialism — Bookchin never in fact deviated from the views he expressed in his earlier writings. Bookchin's core ideas on social ecology, libertarian socialism and libertarian municipalism, which he defended and elaborated on throughout his life, are thus to be found in those key early texts, namely *Post-Scarcity Anarchism*, **Toward an Ecological Society** and his magnus opus *The Ecology of Freedom*.

As Tom Cahill remarked in his generous tribute to Bookchin, these books contain the "essence" of Bookchin's thoughts. Bookchin was therefore not only an important figure in the emergence of the ecology movement, but played an important role, also, as Peter Marshall indicated, in the "renewal" of anarchist theory and practice during the 1970s.

Social Ecology

In the Vatican there is a famous painting by Raphael entitled *The School of Athens*. It depicts Plato as a grey-haired older man pointing to the heavens, while the younger man Aristotle points to the earth. Plato, of course, although having a high regard for mathematics, was fundamentally a religious mystic, a scholar who expressed a dualistic spiritualist metaphysic and had contempt for sensual experience and empirical knowledge. Aristotle, on the other hand, was an empirical naturalist with a deep interest in biology, he described himself as a physikos — one who studies nature. He thus expressed, as Bookchin indicated, an "organic way of thinking."

It has often been said that Western philosophers either side with Plato or with Aristotle. Bookchin clearly sided with the latter, being vehemently opposed to all mystical or theological interpretations of the natural world. Indeed, Alfred Whitehead famously described Western philosophy as merely a series of "footnotes" to Plato.

For all the major figures of the Western philosophical tradition — Aquinas, Descartes, Locke, Leibniz, Kant, Hegel, Husserl, Wittgenstein and Heidegger — were religious thinkers. Bookchin, therefore, very much belonged to a minority tradition within Western philosophy, that of philosophical naturalism.

But what is significant about Raphael's painting is that it reflects the essential paradox at the heart of the human condition. For as scholars such as Lewis Mumford, Edmund Husserl and Erich Fromm have all insisted, humans have, in a sense, a dual existence. For on the one hand humans are earthly beings, and as organisms, intrinsically a part of the natural world.

But on the other hand, humans are a unique species, in having a high degree of self-consciousness and sociality, highly complex symbolic systems and forms of technology that have led recent scholars to suggest that humans have become, in fact, over perhaps the last half century a "geological force" within the "Earth system" itself.

What is significant about Bookchin's philosophical naturalism is that he firmly embraced this "paradox," emphasising that humans were a product of, and had roots in organic evolution, while at the same time, they were animals of a "very special kind." As he expressed it:

> "Human beings are of the biotic world as organisms, mammals and primates, yet they are also apart from it as creatures that produce that vast array of cultural artifacts and associations that we call second nature."

Bookchin therefore expressed like Bakunin and many others a triadic ontology of the human subject, recognising that humans were intrinsically both natural and social beings, as well as having, like other organisms, but in a unique and special way, a sense of self-identity and personhood. The notion that humans are "aliens" or "parasites" on Earth, as suggested by some deep ecologists and acolytes of Nietzsche, Bookchin found quite deplorable. It implies, he argued, the denaturing of humanity and denies the fact that humans are rooted in biology and one of the products of organic evolution.

Bookchin's own metaphysics of nature was a form of evolutionary naturalism, akin to that of Darwin, Marx and Kropotkin. He therefore fervently rejected the two dominant worldviews that had long characterised Western philosophy and culture, namely religion and mechanistic philosophy.

The first of these are the various religious (or mystical) cosmologies — for this worldview has taken a variety of different forms. These include (with the irrespective adherents) tribal animism (or polytheism), Christian theism and goddess religion, panentheism (or theosophy) — which conceives of god as both a transcendent creator and as as manifested in natural phenomena and finally, the various types of mystical pantheism.

The second form of cosmology, that has been dominant in Western culture is the mechanistic worldview that is invariably identified with Rene Descartes. This cosmology expresses a dualistic metaphysic — a radical opposition between humans and nature — an atomistic epistemology, and an anthropocentric ethic that validates the technological domination of nature, and a conception of nature simply as a resource for human use.

Rejecting both ecological mysticism and the mechanistic approach of Cartesian philosophy, Bookchin, in contrast, advocated an organic or evolutionary way of thinking — an ecological worldview that he described as dialectical naturalism (see later).

Although in the broadest sense the term "nature" implies everything that exists, and although this materialist definition may be valid in some respects, Bookchin suggests that this is far too limiting, for nature, from a social ecological perspective, refers to an evolutionary process or development. Bookchin thus defines nature as "a cumulative evolutionary process from the inanimate to the animate and ultimately the social, however differentiated this process may be.

There is a widespread tendency within Western culture, Bookchin argues, to view nature as a realm that is opposed to human freedom and human wellbeing — a realm characterised as "stingy," "intractable," "cruel," and "competitive." It was an image of nature expressed not only by Cartesian philosophy, social Darwinism and the ideology of capitalism (economics in particular) but as Bookchin contends, by Karl Marx.

For Marx conceived of nature as a "realm of necessity" which had to be subdued in order to engender a "realm of freedom." In contrast Bookchin conceives of nature as a gradual, self-developing evolutionary process. Nature therefore is not some divine cosmos nor a lifeless machine, nor could it be equated — as with the deep ecologists — with a pristine wilderness. It is, rather, an evolutionary process of graded and phased development that indicates increasing fecundity, diversity and complexity, and is characterised by the developing of ever-expanding attributes of self-consciousness, subjectivity, creativity and freedom. Following the important studies of Kropotkin and Lynn Margulis Bookchin also contended that nature is characterised not only by conflict and competition but also by co-operation, mutual aid (mutualism) and symbiosis, even between diverse organisms (such as lichen).

Life, therefore, is interactive, procreative, relational and contextual. All life-forms, for Bookchin, even bacteria, exhibit a sense of self-identity and self-maintenance, however germinal and nascent. They therefore have, in varying degrees, subjectivity, self-consciousness, agency and freedom, and are participants in their own evolution.

Bookchin was therefore critical of fashionable neo-Darwinian theory that unduly emphasises the impact of the environment (adaptation) and advocates a gene-centred approach to biology. This approach, Bookchin argued, tends to completely bypass the subjectivity and agency of the organism. Like Brian Goodwin and indeed Darwin, Bookchin advocates an approach to biology that affirms the organism as the fundamental unit of life.

He therefore concluded that within organic evolution there is a striving for greater complexity and increasing degrees of subjectivity (or selfhood) which constitute "the immanent impulse of evolution towards self-awareness."

Bookchin therefore consistently argued that mutualism (co-operation), self consciousness, subjectivity and freedom are inherent tendencies within the natural world. They may, therefore, as potentialities, be realised in human social life, specifically in the creation of an ecological society.

Following a long tradition that goes back to the beginning of Western philosophy, and was well expressed by the Roman scholar Cicero, Bookchin makes a clear distinction (not a dichotomy) between "first nature" and "second nature" the realm of human artifacts, cultural landscapes and of social and symbolic life (1989). But he insists that human social life is "within the realm of nature" and thus always has a naturalistic dimension. The emergence of humans as a life form and of human socio-cultural and symbolic life is, therefore, for Bookchin, a "natural fact" having its roots in biology.

Not only an emergent materialist, Bookchin was fundamentally a social ecologist, and he continuously emphasised the *integrity* of both nature as an objective reality, and human social life. The relationship between nature and human social life is therefore one of *continuity*, a dialectical relationship not one of opposition. Nature is a realm of potentiality for the emergence of human life — in terms of technics, social labour, language, subjectivity — as well as a precondition for the development of society. Bookchin was fond of describing the relationship between humans and (first) nature in terms of a concept derived from Georg Hegel, namely that is a dynamic "unity in diversity."

In an important sense Bookchin, like Lewis Mumford and Rene Dubos, was an ecological humanist, offering a creative synthesis of humanism and naturalism. By humanism, of course, Bookchin meant a shift "in vision from the skies to the earth, from superstition to reason, from deities to people," thereby emphasising the agency and cultural creativity of the human subject — both individually and collectively. Equating humanism with Cartesian philosophy and anthropomorphism as do many deep ecologists and postmodernists, was to Bookchin completely stultifying and obscurantist.

Needless to say secular humanists from Ludwig Feuerbach to Erich Fromm and Lewis Mumford have long critiqued Cartesian metaphysics, emphasising that humans are fundamentally "earthly beings."

In contrast to much social theory and ecological thought, Bookchin put a focal emphasis on both natural and social evolution, on both nature and the integrity of the human species. He was therefore opposed to all dualistic theories that tended to radically bifurcate or separate nature from the social (and spiritual) aspects of human life — as reflected in Platonism, Cartesian theism and other religious cosmologies, as well as in much sociological theory and the humanities. He was especially critical of postmodernism, which tended to ignore biology entirely — though he was mainly concerned with the relativism, misanthropy, a-historicism and nihilism of the likes of Nietzsche and Heidegger.

But Bookchin was equally critical of all forms of reductionism. He was therefore critical of sociobiology, which tended to reduce social life to biology or even to genetics, and of many mystical deep ecologists who tended to address the integrity of the human subject with reference to a universal spiritual "one-ness."

This was akin, he held, to the "night in which all cows are black," Bookchin being fond of quoting Hegel's joking remark on Schelling's mystical idealism. Bookchin, in fact, became a rather maligned figure among many academic philosophers for his trenchant critique of deep ecology even though the substance of this critique was quite compelling.

For Bookchin was critical not just of the eclecticism of the deep ecologists and their tendency to embrace mystical theology — as expressed in Devall and Session's seminal text — but also of their neo-Malthusian tendencies and their emphasis on biocentrism which tended, Bookchin argued, to easily lapse into misanthropy.

In fact, Bookchin was particularly critical of two prominent deep ecologists, Dave Foreman of Earth First! and Christopher Manes who extolled famine in Africa and the AIDs epidemic as acceptable ways of controlling a human population. Such notions deeply disturbed Bookchin, hence the stridency of his polemic.

But Bookchin was also critical of the deep ecologists for holding an undifferentiated humanity responsible for the ecological crisis, when the crisis had its roots in social problems — specifically within the capitalist market economy — thus requiring fundamental social changes and the "remaking" of society.

Bookchin's harsh critique of deep ecology in 1987 generated a heated debate, though the responses to Bookchin's critique and his advocacy of social ecology have tended to verge on caricature.

Dialectical naturalism and ethics

To understand the natural world as an evolutionary process, and the place of humans within the cosmos, Bookchin argued that we need to develop an organic way of thinking, one that is dialectical and processional rather than instrumental, mechanistic and analytical. Such a way of thinking avoids the extremes of both anthropocentrism, exemplified by Cartesian metaphysics and the ideology of capitalism which radically separates humans from nature, and biocentrism, which is a naive form of biological reductionism expressed by mystical deep ecologists. Both approaches, Bookchin felt, expressed a logic of domination, and a hierarchical mindset.

As the philosophy of social ecology therefore advocated a dialectical and evolutionary form of naturalism. It was one that combined and integrated an ecological worldview (naturalism) as a metaphysic of nature (outlined above) with dialectics as a relational epistemology.

To develop a sense of dialectics, Bookchin seems to have immersed himself in the three classical texts on the subject, namely Aristotle's *Metaphysics*, Hegel's *Science of Logic* and Engel's *Dialectic of Nature*. Bookchin fully embraced their dialectical sensibility, but he rejected the theological and teleological aspects of Aristotle's and Hegel's philosophy, emphasising that they lacked an evolutionary perspective, and he felt that Engels was still deeply entrenched in mechanistic materialism, the emphasis being not on development but on matter in motion. Bookchin therefore aimed to develop a dialectical naturalism by "ecologising the dialectic," as he put it in 1995.

A good deal has been written on the subject of dialectics. Some, like Kropotkin, identifying dialectics with Hegel's pantheistic mysticism, have found the concept unhelpful; others have dismissed it as mystical mumbo-jumbo.

What have Galileo's laws of motion and the life-history of an insect to do with dialectics, asked Sidney Hook, whose early writing on Hegel appealed to Bookchin.

Following Karl Popper, anarcho-primitivist Bob Black dismissed dialectics as "mystical gibberish," and, embracing the nihilism of postmodernist theory, dismissed Bookchin as a naive positivist.

Black has thus a rather facile understanding of Bookchin's work, and even less understanding of dialectics, Popper and positivism.

Neither Popper, a critical rationalist and realist, nor Bookchin, a dialectical naturalist, were positivists, Bookchin emphasising that "reality is not simply what we experience" — hardly a positivist sentiment!

What then is dialectics?

Following Engels, three aspects or principles of dialectics may be briefly indicated. The first principle in the understanding of dialectics is the idea that both the natural world and human social life is in a constant state of flux, and that the historical sciences have made the "immutable" concepts of Newton, Descartes and Linnaeus redundant.

The second principle of dialectics emphasises the notion of totality (holism). This is the idea that all the seemingly disparate entities that make up the material world are interconnected, and that no phenomenon (natural or social) can therefore be understood in isolation. As many have expressed it, nature is a complex interactive web.

The final principles of dialectics is expressed by the "paradox," "contradiction," or "units of opposites." Ordinary commonsense understanding, traditional logic, conventional (or instrumental) reason and metaphysical philosophy (especially as expressed by Descartes and Kant) tend to think in terms of "oppositions" rather than dialectically in terms of development and a "unity of opposites." As Engels succinctly described the limitations of metaphysical (non-dialectical) thinking:

> "In the contemplation of individual things, if forgets the connections between them; in a contemplation of their existence, it forgets the beginning and end of their existence; of their repose, it forgets their motion."

As Bookchin conceived it, dialectics was not a form of "logic," nor was it a "method," and it certainly wasn't "mystical gibberish." It was rather a "way of reasoning about reality."

It was then a mode of understanding the world that posited an "emergent" rather than a religious (mystical) or mechanistic way of thinking, that emphasised process and development not simply change or motion, and, finally, that stressed the unity and agency of organisms as well as their complex relationships or interactions.

The conception of nature that Bookchin expressed in many contexts focussed around a number of key concepts. These were:

- ❀ Holism (complexity)
- ❀ Differentiation (diversity)
- ❀ Freedom (subjectivity)
- ❀ Fecundity (creativity)
- ❀ Participation (mutualism)

Nature, therefore, for Bookchin constituted:

> A participatory realm of interactive life forms whose outstanding attributes are fecundity, creativity and directiveness, marked by complementarity that renders the natural world the grounding for an ethics of freedom rather than domination.

As ethics for Bookchin, was an eminently human creation, in that human beings can derive a sense of meaning and value from first nature by virtue of their interpretive powers, then, Bookchin suggested, humanity was the "very *embodiment* of value in nature as a whole." And he goes on to advocate an "ethics of complementarity" which he argued "opposes any claim that human beings have a 'right' to dominate first nature, assuming that they can do so in the first place, much less any claim that first nature has been "created" to serve human needs.

Following in the footsteps of Aristotle, Bookchin sought to promote an ethical naturalism that was consistent with ecological principles and an ecological sensibility.

Arguing against the fact/value dualism of the positivists Bookchin held that first nature may be reasonably regarded as the ground for an ecological ethic. But the natural world itself is not ethical: It is never "cruel" or "kind" or "caring" nor good or bad. Bookchin therefore affirmed that from our knowledge of the natural world, and the place of humans within first nature, humans could thereby derive ethical principles — to guide both human conduct in establishing an ecological community based on the values of co-operation, self-organisation, freedom and diversity.

As an ethical naturalist, like Spinoza and Kropotkin, Bookchin explicitly rejected ethical theories that based moral values simply on tradition or custom (cultural relativism), on subjective whims and individual emotions (as with the logical positivists) or on a "denatured" conception of the human subject (as with Kant).

He was equally critical of all transcendental or absolutist forms of ethics, those which derive moral edicts either from the holy scriptures of Oriental religions (Judaism, Christianity, Islam and Hinduism), mediated of course by clerics, or from the emanations of shamans, charismatic priests or religious gurus, whether enlightened visionaries or messengers of god.

As Bookchin wrote of humans as being "the embodiment of nature rendered self-conscious and self-reflective" and advocated the human "stewardship" of the Earth, and as he stressed the need to go beyond the present dichotomy or rift between first and second natures to create a "free nature," Bookchin has been widely denounced by mystical deep ecologists, anarcho-primitivists and liberal philosophers. He has been accused of being "anthropocentric" and "utilitarian," as advocating a Faustian domination of nature, and as expressing "humanistic arrogance."

These critiques seem to wilfully misinterpret the meanings that Bookchin himself gave to these concepts.

By the "stewardship" of the Earth, Bookchin certainly did not intend to imply that humans should take complete "control" of nature, nor "steer" organic evolution — for Bookchin was an ontological realist, holding that first nature has an independence and integrity quite separate from the human species. What he implied by stewardship was the development of an ecological sensibility that "respects other forms of life for their own sake and responds actively in the form of creative loving and supportive symbiosis.

Likewise, the concept of "free nature" did not imply the "mastery" of nature but but rather the opposite: the greening of the natural world from the plundering of the capitalist system, and the creation of an ecological society in which the relationship between humans and the natural would be one that was co-operative, harmonious and mutualist — a "creative interaction." It would be a society that enhanced the flourishing and wellbeing of *both* the human species and other life forms along with nature itself, a mutuality "between first and second nature that enriched both natures." Bookchin always advocated and stressed an ethics of "complementarity" that is lost on his numerous critics.

Neither indifference, nor the technocratic management of problems within the capitalist system (environmentalism) are viable options to the present social and ecological crisis.

The politics of libertarian socialism

In response to the social and ecological crisis, Bookchin not only insisted on the need to develop a philosophy of dialectical naturalism (a form of ecological humanism) and an ecological sensibility or ethic; he also stressed the need to create — as a radical alternative to liberal capitalism — an ecological society.

He envisaged a rational society based on anarchist principles — a society that was libertarian, socialist, ecological and democratic.

Around 2002, at the age of 81, he announced that he had ceased to define himself as an anarchist, leading Iain McKay to later suggest that Bookchin in his last years had attempted to "trash his own legacy." But it is important to recognise that the anarchism Bookchin abandoned was what he had earlier rejected, in a harsh polemic, as "lifestyle" anarchism. This kind of anarchism, otherwise known as "post-left anarchy" or by academic scholars as the "new" anarchism, consists of a motley collection of distinct strands, among them Stirnerite egoism (Jason McQuinn), Nietzschean aesthetic individualism (Hakim Bey), anarcho-primitivist (John Zerzan et al), post-anarchism, and at the extremes the "anarcho" capitalism of Ayn Rand and Murray Rothbard.

Anarchism as a political tradition has usually been defined in several ways.

The first, well exemplified by Peter Marshall's history of anarchism, conceives of it in terms of an opposition to coercive authority, specifically as being "anti-State." Thus an extremely wide variety of philosophies and individuals have been described as anarchists — Godwin, Stirner, religious mystics like Tolstoy or Gandhi, radical libertarians, mutualists, anarcho-capitalists as well as many anarcho-communists. Even Margaret Thatcher and the authoritarian Marxist Che Guevara find a place in Marshall's important survey of anarchism.

This has enabled liberal and Marxist scholars to dismiss anarchism as a completely incoherent philosophy.

It isn't. For there is a second way of understanding anarchism, and this is to view it as fundamentally a historical social movement and political movement that emerged only around 1870, mainly among working-class members of the First International. This form of anarchism, as many scholars have emphasised, combined the ideas of both radical liberalism with its emphasis on liberty and individual freedom, and socialism (or communism) with its emphasis on equality, voluntary associations, mutual aid and direct action.

This unity, which indeed defines anarchism as libertarian socialism, was most succinctly expressed in the well-known adage of Michael Bakunin:

"That liberty without socialism is privilege and injustice, and that socialism without liberty is slavery and brutality."

In his polemic *Listen Marxist!* Bookchin has critiqued Marxism for its lack of a libertarian perspective, while his later polemic *Social Anarchism or Lifestyle Anarchism* critiqued a wide variety of contemporary anarchists (noted above) for their bourgeois individualism and for lacking a socialist perspective. Thus anarcho-communism, social anarchism, libertarian socialism and communalism are virtual synonyms, different expressions of Bookchin's political philosophy of anarchism.

Thus it is important to recognise that throughout his life, and even in his last years, Bookchin remained true to the legacy of St Imier — a committed and strident libertarian socialist.

The lifestyle anarchists, as Bookchin described them — the Nietzscheans, Stirnerites and primitivists especially — not only rejected socialism (and society) but went to extremes and rejects civilisation (even agriculture and human language), technology and city life. What is important about Bookchin is that he attempted to avoid these extremes, and like Lewis Mumford, was never anti-civilisation, anti-technology or anti-city. To the contrary, he affirmed all three as vital creative aspects of the human spirit. Alive to the achievement of human civilisation, Bookchin completely rejected anarcho-primitivism.

In his *Ecology of Freedom* Bookchin devotes a chapter to what he described as "organic society," the early hunter-gatherers and tribal societies. He describes the "outlook" of such societies as having the following features: A form of equality and an absence of coercive and domineering values, a feeling of unity between the individual and their community, a sense of common property with an emphasis on mutual aid and usufruct rights, and finally an ecological sensibility, involving a relationship with the world that was one of reciprocal harmony, not of domination.

But like Kropotkin, Bookchin was only too aware of the limitations of tribal life, and was therefore concerned that we we draw inspiration and lessons from the past, and from previous cultures, rather than romanticising them. Still less should we try to emulate them. Given the present human population, the "future primitive" of John Zerzan is simply not a political option.

Although Bookchin was always a harsh critic of anarcho-primitivism, he was not an obsessive "technocrat" as David Watson portrays him. Nor was he besotted with civilisation. He certainly emphasised the importance of city life, especially in introducing the idea of a common humanity, a universal *humanitas*, but like Kropotkin and Mumford — both important influences on Bookchin — and unlike the anarcho-primitivists, Bookchin had a much more nuanced approach to technology and civilisation. As he put it his pro-technology stand:

"Which is not to deny that many technologies are inherently domineering and ecologically dangerous or to assert that civilisation has been an unmitigated blessing. Nuclear reactors, huge dams, highly centralised industrial complexes, the factory system and the arms industry — like bureaucracy, urban blight and contemporary media — have been pernicious almost from their inception."

~ *Social Anarchism or Lifestyle Anarchism*

Technology, Bookchin felt, had to become "liberatory" and be reduced to a "human scale" and through the Institute of Social Ecology, co-founded with Dan Chodorkoff, he pioneered the use of renewable energy sources, and promoted organic farming.

Following Kropotkin, Bookchin comes to emphasise that there has been two sides to human history — a legacy of domination reflected in the emergence of hierarchy, State power and capitalism and a legacy of freedom, reflected in the history of ever-expanding struggles for emancipation.

In order to to develop libertarian municipalism as an integral part of or strategy of anarchism (communalism) Bookchin, in his extensive writings, described in detail the many forms of popular assemblies that had emerged in the course of European history, particularly during times of social revolution. Bookchin was particularly enthusiastic with respect to the Athenian polis and its system of direct democracy — though recognising its historical context and its limitations. But forms of popular democracy have occurred throughout history, and Bookchin described in particular the popular assemblies of medieval towns, the neighbourhood sections during the French Revolution, the Paris Commune of 1871, the workers' soviets during the Russian Revolution and the New England town meetings, as well as the anarchist collectives during the Spanish Civil War of the 1930s.

In his later essays Bookchin came to explicitly distinguish between four radical political traditions, namely marxism, anarcho-syndicalism, anarchism (equated with lifestyle anarchism) and communalism or libertarian socialism.

Always critical of Marxism, or what is termed "proletarian socialism" Bookchin rejected the notion that the industrial proletariat could any longer be conceived as the "hegemonic historical agent" in the struggle against capitalism, given the fundamental social and technological changes that had taken place within global capitalism during the second half of the 20th century. He was equally critical of the Marxist emphasis on the State, whether this implied working through the bourgeois democratic State or adopting the strategy of the Bolsheviks during the Russian Revolution.

Bookchin was also critical of revolutionary or anarcho-syndicalism with its strategic focus on the industrial worker and the factory system. Although acknowledging their libertarian bias, Bookchin rejects the workerist emphasis of the syndicalists and laments their lack of a coherent theory.

It has therefore been suggested by many scholars that Bookchin ignored the importance of class, and that the concept of labour virtually disappears his social ecology, even though the workplace remains a critical site of capitalist exploitation. But in fact Bookchin never repudiates the concept of class, nor the importance of class analysis. He always acknowledged the crucial importance of the working class in achieving any form of social revolution, and categorically affirmed the importance of the class struggle.

But given his emphasis on advancing the "communalist project" as the socialism of the 21st century, class issues nevertheless do seem to be side-tracked.

As articulated earlier, Bookchin's polemical essay *Social Anarchism or Lifestyle Anarchism* was essentially a defence of libertarian socialism, offering a trenchant critique of several anarchist tendencies that were prominent in the 1990s — specifically Nietzschean poetic terrorism (so called), anarcho-primitivism and Stirnerite egoism. Labelling them lifestyle anarchism, what linked these various tendencies for Bookchin was their affirmation of a radical individualism that gave absolute priority to an unfettered, autonomous ego.

For Bookchin, none of these currents of thought articulated an authentic political theory — one based on democratic self-management of the municipality.

Unlike Nietzschean "free spirits" and Stirnerite individualists, who in elitist fashion rely on other mortals to provide them with the basic necessities of life, Bookchin recognised that throughout human history some form of social organisation has always been evident, for humans are intrinsically social beings, not autonomous possessives egos. Some kind of organisation has therefore always been essential not only in terms of human survival, but specifically in terms of the care and upbringing of children (kinship), in the production of food, shelter and clothing, and the basic necessities of social life (the social economy) and, finally, in the management of human affairs, relating to community decisions and the resolution of conflicts (politics).

Bookchin, therefore, was always keen to distinguish between ordinary social life — focussed around family life and kinship, affinity groups, various cultural associations and productive activities — and the political life of a community, focused around local assemblies.

Bookchin was equally insistent on distinguishing between politics — which he defined as a theory relating to a public realm and those social institutions by means of which people democratically manage their community affairs — and what he called statecraft. The latter was focused on the State as a form of government that served as an instrument for class exploitation, oppression and control.

Bookchin thus came to put an emphasis on the need to establish popular democratic assemblies based on the municipality, on neighbourhoods, towns or villages. Such local assemblies, through face-to-face democracy, would make policy decisions relative to the management of community affairs.

He argued consistently that such decisions should be made by majority vote, though Bookchin does not advocate majority rule, and emphasised that a free society would only be one that fosters the fullest degree of dissent and liberty. Municipalities would be linked through a confederate political system. He warned, however, of the dangers of the assembly becoming an "incipient State."

Bookchin expressed his own conception of anarchist politics in terms of four central tenets: "A confederation of decentralised municipalities, an unwavering opposition to Statism, a belief in direct democracy and a vision of a libertarian communist society."

Murray Bookchin of course did not provide us with all the answers to our current problems: To the contrary he left us with many unresolved issues. Exactly what kinds of technology do we need to sustain or develop; what exactly is involved in decentralising the urban landscape, and what precisely is the relationship between community politics and class struggles focused on the workplace are, for example, all unresolved issues for contemporary radicals.

In an era when corporate capitalism still reigns triumphant, creating conditions of political turmoil and social dislocation, and severe ecological problems, particularly that of global warming, we surely need to take seriously Bookchin's legacy.

In a fine biography of Bookchin, Janet Biehl described him in his last years as being rather like a whale stranded on the beach. This may well be true, but Bookchin's creative synthesis of socialism, dialectical naturalism and libertarian social ecology was a truly outstanding contribution to radical philosophy, and as a conceptual resource it has an enduring value.

THE APPLE FALLS FROM GRACE
by Chris Wilbert

The History and Changing Meaning of the Apple as a Cultivated Fruit; Changing Attitudes towards nature from Ancient Societies to the Present Day

1. Introduction

The Apple perhaps more than any other fruit has been intimately bound up with humans. Thoreau called the Apple tree "the most civilised of all trees" being longer cultivated than any other and so more humanised.[7] This relationship has been shown in many ways. In Ancient cultures, such as the Greeks, Romans, and Celts, the Apple was the source of much folklore, magic and symbolism, which reflected the values and worldview of the cultures themselves.

As human society has changed, so too has the relationship between humans and nature, in this sense historical and cultural change leads to ecological and social change,[8] and these changes can be seen in the way that fruits and other crops are grown. In this way the Apple is used here partly as a metaphor for nature as a whole.

The changes of the fourteenth century onwards, the rise of capitalism, the scientific revolution and the fusion of science and capitalism has taken the Apple from a fruit imbued with spiritual and symbolic meaning — the fruit of health and immortality — to a fruit given only a single function, that of production of profit and a fruit feared because of the chemicals that are applied to it. Now genetic engineering promises to make the Apple almost unrecognisable as a Tree, in the drive to increase production, standardisation and remove labour costs.

The old symbolism has not completely gone however, instead it too has been commodified and now adorns the "industries of the new age," Apple Computers being but one example.

In these ways capitalism has separated us from the source and knowledge of production of essentials such as food, we are encouraged to trust the experts who are motivated mainly by profits[9] and we are learning that we should not. Without such knowledge of production for food, no moral responsibility for social and environmental consequences of one's decisions of what to buy seems possible.[10]

Alternatives do exist, and ways of breaking out of this impersonal, morally irresponsible system, to bring the knowledge and meaning of food production and nature back into our lives, can and must be found. These cannot be separated from wider political realities however, nor should it be seen that to go back to some mythical golden age is the answer. But we can learn from the past by seeing what has been and what has gone wrong and look to a future to see what can be.

2. Fruit Cultivation: Myth, Magic and Folk Symbols

In the essential prose
of things, the Apple Tree
stands up, emphatic
among the accidents of the afternoon, solvent
not to be denied.[11]

Wild fruits have probably always been collected by humans and still are, the Apple was particularly valued for its nutritional and storable qualities, and because it can be dried and kept over winter.[12] Cultivation of the Apple probably dates back to the Stone Age[13] and most likely began in the area of the Caucasus and Northern India where forests of wild Apples are found.[14] The Apple was cultivated in Egypt in the twelfth century BC and the Greeks and Romans were also adept at grafting and propagation of Apple trees. The Roman Palladius wrote of thirty-seven varieties in the fourth century BC.

It is not known whether the apple was cultivated in Britain before the Romans invaded, though the crab apple (Malus sylvestris) is native and was highly valued by the Celts.

The Romans did introduce their own form of fruit cultivation but after they left little is known of fruit growing in Britain until the Norman invasion apart from a few scattered references to orchards in monasteries.[15] There is only one reference to an orchard in the Domesday Book; however it is thought that this reflects the commonplace nature of fruit growing on an individual basis rather than as a co-operative pursuit.[16]

Trees have played an important part in the spiritual history of most cultures and trees bearing life-foods were always sacred.[17] It is probable that humans in an early stage of civilisation, living a hard life close to nature, constructed no definite philosophy of life that could explain all the phenomena or workings of nature with which they came into contact. Their "rude" science thus explained itself largely in satisfying their simple wants and needs in warding off dangers and appeasing the wrath of evil powers.[18] In such communities the natural world was viewed in anthropomorphic terms, spirits permeated matter, such that the earth was seen as animate,[19] a living organism and nurturing mother, and this view served as a cultural constraint restricting the exploitative action of humans.[20] Within such a cosmology, nothing was seen as isolated and apart, but in its relation to the whole of life, of which each object formed an integral part.[21] Thus, everyday things were invested with a deep symbolism or cosmological significance.[22] This paganism or animism was to some extent incorporated within Christianity when it arrived in Europe and Britain, but a marked shift did occur with nature being seen as man's (sic) dominion and thus separate from nature.

One of the most widely known mentions of the apple in myth is the Christian story of the Garden of Eden in which Adam and Eve partake of the Fruit of the Tree of Knowledge of Good and Evil, which is most commonly seen as the Apple,[23] and are then cast out of the Garden of Innocence by God into the world of experience. Russell has interpreted this myth, along with similar other ones from other cultures along with anthropological studies of societies in Papua New Guinea, as being connected with Kinship. She arrives at some significant conclusions in connection with fruit trees:

From evidence about modern societies that practice simple farming, I was able to show that the fruit tree is the oldest form of property fixed to a place, and the theft of fruit the oldest form of crime in farming societies (the original sin). Moreover, since fruit trees may last more than a generation, the fruit tree is the oldest form of heritable fixed property. Since it is important that fruit trees be cared for, it becomes important to control and certify kinship succession. Hence the fruit tree gives rise to the family tree. At this stage of cultural evolution, to ensure regular kinship succession, mating regulations begin to be connected with property.[24]

Thus, in Eden mating regulations are broken, the Tree of Life may be said to represent stable succession of inheritance (immortality), which ensures a kind of eternal life and renewal for the trees and those who succeed in tending them. The story of Eden may therefore be telling of the expulsion of groups who infringed the rules of mating.[25]

As the classical symbol of youth and renewal the apple naturally rated high in Greek mythology. The apple was a bridal symbol and offering, sacred to Venus as love and desire.[26] The apple being round in shape, like many fruits, represents totality and unity and is sacred to Apollo the Sun god[27] (Ibid), while the Temple of Artemis was within an orchard.[28]

In Celtic mythology, the apple was one of the central life trees of the Gaelic elysium,[29] seen as the Silver Bough, it has magic and cthonic powers, it is the emblem of security,[30] immortality and the fruit of the other world: The apple was the talisman which led him into the world of the immortals and fed him with the fruit of life and everlasting happiness.[31]

The druids planted apple trees in sacred places for their fruit and as harbours for mistletoe which was also sacred to them.[32] Hallowe'en is the Celtic apple festival which marks the celebration of the beginning of winter and death of the old year — on the eve of November 1st. This was also the eve of New Year's Day in Anglo-Saxon times and this date was also dedicated to the spirit which presides over fruit and seeds.[33]

On Twelfth Night, which has absorbed many early hallowe'en customs many folkrites were also carried out by people in orchards. One such is apple wassailing which took place in Cornwall, Devon and Somerset. On this night parishioners walk in procession visiting the main orchards in the parish. In each orchard one tree is selected and saluted with an incantation, the tree is then sprinkled with cider to ensure it bears plentifully the ensuing year. Implements are then banged to drive out evil spirits and arouse the tree spirits. "Hail to thee, good apple tree, pocket-fulls, hat-fulls, peck-fulls, bushel-bag fulls" goes one version of this Wassailing chorus. Afterwards vast quantities of cider are consumed.[34] The apple was also associated in many cultures with health and healing; King Arthur's grievous wound was treated in the Vale of Avalon, the Apple Vale of Celtic myth.[35] Fruit trees were also planted in many places upon the birth of a new child and the health of the tree was thought to reflect that of the child.[36]

Another famous myth has it that one day while sitting in an orchard an apple fell and hit Isaac Newton (the "father" of modern physics) upon the head and that this gave him the inspiration for his Law of Gravity. The irony of this story is that Newton was one of the most important formulators of the mechanistic view of nature. In conjunction with, and to some extent as a result of, the increased exploitation of the earth under early capitalism, this new paradigm of scientific thought eroded the view of nature as being in a generalised sense female, alive and responsive to human action and acting as a normative restraint on human exploitation. The new mechanistic theories and capitalism, morally underpinned by contemporary Christian theology, replaced this with a view of nature as an inanimate, dead, physical system over which "man" (sic) had dominion. This, as we shall see, had far reaching effects in the way humans exploit nature.

3. The Apple and the Rising Market System

The transformation from feudalism to capitalism set in motion a number of changes which eventually affected every form of life in Western societies.

When we look at these historical changes in human impact on the system as a whole, we can see that historical change becomes ecological change due to the "dynamic interactions of the natural and cultural subsystems."[38]

The main factor in the transformation of the early modern period was the growth in the market system for food production and other goods, such as wool, based on property rights and exchanges in land and money. This, along with population increases and urbanisation, advances in agricultural improvement and the growth of rural industry, gradually broke down communal farming practices that were part of the feudal system.[38] People's experiences of an increasingly manipulated nature also undermined the organic worldview and made way for the mechanistic model which reinforced and accelerated the exploitation of nature and human beings as resources.[39] While the spreading use of money facilitated open-ended accumulation of capital as opposed to the somewhat more limited feudal aim of production for consumption (including conspicuous consumption).[40] In these ways (and others) production for subsistence was replaced by rationally maximising modes of economic organisation for the market.

The tendency towards growth, expansion and accumulation in capitalism led to continued displacement of subsistence farmers,[41] the growth of waged labour and the bringing into cultivation of new lands by improvement and reclamation as well as by enclosure of common lands.[42] This process was aided by new books in the 16th and 17th centuries on agricultural improvements (in a scientific sense) and in the case of fruit, instructions on ordering, grafting and propagation.[43] These early changes were essentially focussed around London being the largest urban market and in this it is worth remembering the words of Hughes: "It is significant that the first urban societies were also the first societies to abandon a religious attitude of oneness with nature and to adopt one of separation."[44]

4. Transformations in Fruit Cultivation

Norman London, according to a contemporary account, was full of citizens gardens and orchards. All the main monasteries, encouraged to be self-sufficient since the time of St Benedict,[45] at Whitefriars, Blackfriars, Charterhouse and Holborn had their own gardens in which fruit was grown.[46] In the 13th century fruit was extensively grown in the Royal Gardens at Tower Hill and Westminster.[47] But fruit growing was not confined to the rich and monastic orders, though few records survive of peasant cultivation, Langland in Piers Ploughman of 1,362 mentions that the poor ate baked apples and cherries.[48]

Surplus fruits from the monasteries and Royal gardens, and from the Manor farming systems were sold at the "Market Cross" at this time and this sale of fruit and other crops became so profitable that the system of renting gardens and orchards to grow especially for market became established.[49] This market gardening first developed in and around London in the late thirteenth and fourteenth centuries.[50]

Cantor states that because this was a small-scale affair it was well suited to peasants with plenty of family labour, producing vegetables in beds separated by fruit trees and supplemented by produce from communal fields. By 1650 however a class of wealthy market gardeners emerged who acquired larger holdings and whose soil they improved with fertilisers and employed wage earners of displaced peasants to work them.[51] Specialised fruit production was already well established in Kent by the end of the 15th century also supplying the markets of London. Jordan states that this required very heavy and certainly very profitable capital outlay.[52]

Herefordshire, Worcestershire, Somerset and Devon were also becoming main fruit growing areas, tending to focus more on cider production due to poorer transport and smaller markets.[53] Each of these areas had their own local varieties such as Cornish Aromatic, Hereford Pearmain, Flower of Kent and Devonshire Quarrenden, as well as growing more widespread varieties such as Golden Pippin.

Until the 16th century fruit growing in Britain had changed little from how it was undertaken in Greek or Roman times, apart from becoming somewhat more intensive. However, at this time new developments came about which signalled the move towards increasing economic rationalisation.

The first of these was the introduction of dwarfing rootstocks from France, called "Paradise." These enabled more trees to be planted in an area than before. Legendre, in his book *The Manner of Ordering Fruit Trees* (translated in 1660) suggested these should be spaced six to nine feet apart, instead of the 18–24 feet for trees on seedlings.[54] This practice of dwarfing trees prevented the undercropping of other plants beneath the trees which had previously been widespread and marks the beginning of the transformation of the apple tree to fit economic "needs" of humans.

The developing mechanistic worldview, which saw nature as disorder and cultivation as the imposition of human order was distinguished by increasingly regular planting forms and monocultures, and an increasing admiration of it. None was more admired than the Quincunx, the old Roman way of setting out an orchard.[55] Thus, in the time of Henry VIII, Richard Harris planted over 100 acres of fruit trees at Teynham, Kent: "So beautifully as they not only stand in most right lines, but seem to be of one sort, shape and fashion."[56]

Increased planting of orchards continued in the 18th century, supplied by many new nurseries especially around London. However, the increased acreage of orchards and the monocultural system began to have adverse side-effects by the late 18th century, with large-scale devastation by pests and diseases, as a result of the disruption of ecosystem balances. Canker and Woolly Aphid — introduced on dwarfing rootstocks — became rife, fruit quality and yields became very poor.[57] These problems led to more attention being given to possible remedies by the likes of the newly-formed Royal Horticultural Society, rather than any basic questioning of their causes.

By the middle of the 18th century, English agriculture was well on the way to becoming a fully commercial activity, organised and administered according to the needs of the market,[58] and dominated by the triple divisions into landlords, tenant farmers and hired labourers.[59]

In the 19th century few new developments came about in fruit cultivation. However, fruit growing continued to intensify under the influence of rapid population growth and urbanisation, increasing per capita incomes, cheaper transport costs and more integrated markets. At the same time French imports of apples and high sugar prices caused periodic contractions in cultivation.[60]

At this time many apple varieties grown today were introduced, these often having arisen as chance seedlings, Bramleys Seedling, Cox's Orange Pippin, and Worcester Pearmain being examples.[61] The next set of new developments in fruit cultivation did not come about until the early 20th century with the integration of science into commercial fruit production.

5. The Apple as a Machine

Most developments and improvements in fruit cultivation before the twentieth century came from individual growers and gardeners, amateur "Scientists" and particularly in the 19th century from commercial nurseries such as Laxtons of Bedford.[62] By the early 20th century however, research into new varieties by nurseries was largely given up as the new scientific research stations, financed by growers and government took a leading role[63] and a more scientific management of commercial orchards came into being.

The setting up of fruit research stations, principally those at Long Ashton, Bristol in 1903 (initially as the Cider Institute) and East Mailing, Kent in 1913, can be seen as part of the more general "scientific-technical revolution," in which science became directly organised and dominated by capitalist institutions and was placed at the centre of production.[64] This process of integration is described by Braverman:

Science is the last — and after labour the most important — social property to be turned into an adjunct of capital... At first science costs the capitalist nothing, since he merely exploits the accumulated knowledge of the physical sciences, but later the capitalist systematically organises and harnesses science, paying for scientific education, research, laboratories etc, out of the huge surplus social product which either belongs directly to him or which the capitalist class as a whole controls in the form of tax revenues. A formerly relatively free-floating social endeavour is integrated into production and the market.[65]

The mechanistic philosophy and reductionist method of science harmonised well with the expanding capitalist system into a rationalised system of scientific management, in which the most efficient, scientifically and logically based means are sought to achieve pre-determined capitalist ends.[66] Thus, in the scientific-technical revolution, scientific management sets itself the problem of grasping the process of production as a whole and controlling every element of it, without exception. As H L Gantt wrote:

Improving the system of management means the elimination of elements of chance or accident and the accomplishment of all the ends desired in accordance with knowledge derived from a scientific investigation of everything down to the smallest details of labour.[67]

The result of this approach is that commercial fruit production has been revolutionised and has followed the precepts of rationalisation apparent in other industries and agricultural sectors. Fruit growers have become ever more specialised, landholdings have become bigger, more capital intensive and more incorporated into sectors of the chemical, engineering and food processing industries.[68]

These developments have been made possible by the scientific investigations of the fruit research stations, much of it sponsored by companies such as ICI, Monsanto, Ciba-Geigy Agrochemicals, J Sainsbury Pic, Hoechst, and of course The Ministry of Agriculture, Fisheries and Food (MAFF) who are the main sponsors.[69] MAFF grants are not given unless it can be shown that the research is of "practical" importance and the current government's policy is emphasising this by cutting financial support for East Mailing and other research stations, so that a higher proportion of funding comes from the private sector and is thus more market orientated.[70]

Currently, control of Apple production is mainly focussed on chemicals and hybridisation, though this is shifting towards what is seen as the "ultimate" control of the apple, through genetic engineering. Up to twelve chemicals and hormones can be applied to apples in a single season,[71] rich pickings indeed for the chemical companies. These are applied to apples at almost every stage of growth from beginning to end. They are used to control pests and diseases (of which there are an increasing number due to further disruption of predator-prey relationships), to thin fruit out on the tree, to control growth, to "stick" apples to the tree and prevent windblow losses, to prevent rotting in storage and to lengthen shelf life. This is a potent cocktail synergistically speaking, yet what inadequate testing does take place is only to define lethal doses, not how chemicals may work together or effects of long term low level exposures.

Already several fungicides used regularly in the fruit industry, such as Mancozeb, Captan, and Folpet, are known carcinogens.[72] But most menacing are the growth regulators such as Alar (daminozide), which are used to slow the growth of leaves and branches on trees, and thus force an increase in budding and fruit production. These regulators and some herbicides dramatically alter growth rates at the level of the individual cell.[73] Alar sales were stopped in the US because of links with cancer in young children and caused storms of protest from farmers and industry with the decision being roundly condemned by the Wall Street Journal as: "false or superficial science prevailing over the real thing."[74] A similar controversy erupted in Britain over the US decision, but after a brief review, the government decided in December 1989 that all daminozide based products (Alar and Dazide) were safe.[75]

Developments in plant breeding have also led to more intensive planting systems with even more dwarfing trees. These can be as little as 1 metre in height, while some bush trees need to be permanently staked and their branches strung up because they cannot support themselves. These developments allow labour "maintenance and picking" costs to be reduced. Attempts to mechanise harvesting altogether are at present limited to fruit for cider or juice due to damage to the fruit.[76] Though fully automated chemical sprayers have recently been developed.[77] Recent research has turned to genetic control of apple characteristics. Here, by mapping genes responsible for control of tree habit, pest and disease resistance, and fruit characteristics, genes will be selected and transferred to give the right requirements for high yields, pest resistance and early cropping, this "will allow the normally slow process of conventional breeding to be accelerated."[78]

So far this has resulted in the new columnar varieties, compact, branchless "trees" which have taken thirty years to develop. They require no pruning, crop early, need very little space and are thus being marketed under the legend: "Now even the smallest garden can have an orchard."[79]

These mutations however, bear little relation to a tree at all, having been stripped down to a purely functional level. Like the dwarf varieties of commercial orchards, they have no meaning beyond a straight economic one.

The effects of increasing economic rationalisation have also been evident in the numbers of varieties grown commercially and available in shops. Over 6,000 varieties of apple are known, yet modern commercial orchards are dominated by only nine varieties.[80]

English orchards are dominated by Cox's Orange Pippin and its coloured forms, making up 63% of dessert apple production in 1986, while Bramleys Seedlings made up 90% of culinary apples.[81] Only another six or seven dessert apples are widely available; most of these being imported often from as far away as Canada or New Zealand.

This increasing specialisation in only a few varieties is a relatively recent trend of the twentieth century. In 1917, Prothero could boast that as many as 200 varieties of apple were collected in a single orchard,[82] now he would be lucky to find more than two or three varieties in most orchards. This loss of local varieties of apples that were often intimately related to their area can be seen as yet another factor in the loss of distinctiveness and identification of regions that has followed from the application of scientific management to agriculture.[83]

The work of the orchard labourer has also been transformed, with developments to reduce "maintenance" and harvesting labour costs becoming increasingly deskilled and seasonally intense. Little information about these changes is available however, with only brief references in works such as Ronald Blythe's Akenfield. The older orchard workers spoken to in connection with this research all bemoaned the lack of activity of most of the year and the much more intense and fast harvesting season in comparison to earlier days when the job was more varied, skilled and spread more evenly throughout the year.[84]

The sorting of fruit is now carried out on factory production line systems in on-farm refrigerated stores which are usually run on a co-operative basis between local farmers. Here the fruit is sorted into its various classes under EC quality standards and the Agricultural Development and Advisory Services Fruit Group provides advice to employers on how to run these lines on strict "time and motion" systems to get the best results from the mainly female, part-time and low-paid workforce.

6. The Commodification of Apple Symbolism

As society has changed, the old symbols of ancient and pre-modern cultures have to a great extent lost their meaning[85] and have been replaced by new symbols that reflect the surroundings of contemporary, materialistic culture. Yet as Cooper states, a large body of symbolism has become traditional over the ages and this constitutes an international language transcending the normal limits of communication.[86]

It may be that this traditional form of symbolism (which is most often nature symbolism and includes the apple) is selectively commodified by capitalism, in that it is used to imbue or associate technologies, goods and services with symbolic qualities of other phenomena, to make products more attractive to buyers. For example the apple is used by Apple computers and for Midland Bank's orchard account, amongst others. This can be seen as a marketing or advertising ploy to associate these products with the traditional symbolic qualities of the apple, of health, wisdom and fertility, as well as the naturalism and simplicity of the Apple to make these products and services more appealing and more saleable.

This use can also be seen in the gardens of the early twentieth century suburban estates of London and other cities. Here apple, pear and plum trees were often planted by builders, possibly to accentuate the rustic feeling of these areas. For as Jackson notes, a major attraction of suburban life had always been the opportunity it seemed to offer of enjoying the pleasanter aspects of rural life whilst remaining in touch with the amenities of urban civilisation.[87] Some of these estates, as they spread further out into the countryside, were actually built on old orchards and some trees were left in place as at Broadlands estate, Ponders End in North London.[88]

Though it is easy to mock or denigrate this using of fruit trees in the suburbs, as Ward states, English gardens often remain a haven for the older fruit varieties no longer grown commercially.[89] For example, Hampstead Garden Society boasts over 80 apple varieties in its members" gardens.

7. Futures

As we have seen, it is the nature of our current economic and social system which reduces the apple to a commodity with a single function. This has led to the transformation of the apple tree to meet the needs of capitalist production, a process which has mainly taken place in the horticultural research stations. It is clear that big business — particularly chemical companies — do well out of this research, yet what does the customer, the buyer of apples receive in return for the huge amount of public investment? Cheaper apples perhaps, but we also get a smaller choice of apple varieties; "most" people seem to think we get apples that no longer taste much at all, and we get apples that are sprayed with innumerable hazardous chemicals.

Such developments are leading to a greater questioning of how far we can trust food producers, chemical companies etc, when their motive is profits.

Yet things do not have to be this way. The apple need not be confined to massive orchards, as staked up, chemically soaked bush trees. In Switzerland for example, as I was informed by a research scientist from East Mailing, there seems to be a move to take a broader view of fruit cultivation. Instead of following a policy of transforming the apple tree to fit economic needs, fruit cultivation was being seen as part of the workings and aesthetics of the wider landscape and this was leading to a more "traditional" form of cultivation.

Nor should we rely on private gardens in Britain, as a refuge for varieties not commercially available. As Alexander states:

> Fruit trees on common land add much more to the neighbourhood and the community than the same trees in private backyards: privately grown, the trees tend to produce more fruit than one household can consume. On public land, the trees concentrate the feeling of mutual benefit and responsibility. And because they require yearly care, pruning and harvesting the fruit trees naturally involve people in their common land.[90]

The idea of community orchards, like the aim of growing one's own food (or at least a portion of it), aiming at buying fewer environmentally and socially destructive products, and insisting on organic foods, can be seen as an attempt to achieve some form of moral responsibility for one's economic decisions in the market.

As Tisdell has noted, the market system operates in a way that minimises the amount of knowledge needed to make an economic decision. As the divided responsibility of production has led to divided responsibility for its social and environmental impacts, so the overall lack of knowledge arising out of the market system has further diminished the moral responsibility for these impacts. For example, when one buys apples one need only know the price and quality of apples. No knowledge is required of the producer, the production process or its social and environmental impacts (both of production and consumption). Yet without such knowledge, says Tisdell, no moral responsibility for environmental consequences of one's decisions seems possible. Even if knowledge is available, the remoteness of production may reduce any feeling of responsibility for social and environmental effects.[91]

It is this moral void which lies at the heart of capitalist society. As Jones states, in his discussion of Weber, this is a function of the fragmentation of reason, whereby reason is constrained to seek the most efficient, scientifically and logically based means to achieve pre-determined ends. This formal rationality therefore does not extend our vision or grasp of meaning in the world:

> On the contrary, the myth, legend, folklore, poetry and magic, necessary for the creation of ultimate meanings in human societies and the emergence of a holistic worldview are rejected.[92]

Seen in this way it is evident that capitalism and its scientifically backed formal rationality, cannot solve the current, and growing, social and environmental problems. The problems emanate from the system itself. Nor can going back to a cosmological view be an answer, such philosophies were long ago destroyed by mechanistic science. Only with an ecological way of thinking and acting which posits humanity as inseparable from nature can these problems be properly addressed. If this is fully understood "...it will no longer be possible for us to injure nature wantonly, as this would mean injuring an integral part of ourselves."[93]

Such a move may seem far off today. Yet much can and is being done to educate people, and to encourage awareness of the more manifold meanings of nature, especially in urban areas which remain so alienated from nature and alienating for people.

There is no reason for example, why we should not have "real" apple trees and other fruits growing all over our cities. As Alexander states:

> The presence of orchards adds an experience that has all but vanished from our cities — the experience of growth, harvest, local sources of fresh food; walking down a city street pulling an apple out of a tree and biting into it.[94]

Appleyard quotes the example of Chandigarh, the capital of India's Punjab, where the main roads of the city are lined with peaches and plum trees.[95] In Nanking in China, one sixth of trees planted in the city are fruit bearing, including lychees and mangoes.[96] There are problems of course in the amount of pollution from cars etc, in cities, but fruit growing can help draw more attention to this pollution.

The main tree identified with London is the London Plane (Platanus x acerifolia), a tree of uncertain origin, large, unusual, but purely a decorative tree. The plane tree is also symbolic of moral superiority.[97] How much better to have the apple tree, in its many forms, growing all over London again. Symbolic of health, immortality, love and fertility — these are qualities our towns and cities should seek to emulate.

Appendix

The original interest in this subject came from the "Save Old Orchards" campaign run by the environmental arts group Common Ground. In 1988 a short project was carried out by myself at Thames Polytechnic into attitudes to, and uses of, fruit grown in people's gardens. This research threw up many more questions than it answered, but the background knowledge gained then, has added much to this research.

Part one of this paper dealing with mythology and symbolism was researched mainly at the Folklore Library, University College and relies extensively on the 1928 work by Eleanor Hull, who truly seems to have loved the symbolism surrounding apples. Much more remains to be discovered on this subject however.

The history of fruit cultivation is well covered by F A Roach, but coming from an ex-director of East Mailing research station, reflects a very pro-scientific view regarding developments. In reviewing the history I have followed Carolyn Merchant's method that historical change becomes ecological change, emphasising human impact on the system as a whole, whilst using the Apple as an example. As she rightly points out, Natural and Cultural subsystems are in dynamic interaction and cannot be separated.

The modern developments in fruit cultivation are by no means dealt with exhaustively, there being so many. It has also been hard to find works to explain adequately the mind-boggling nature of some of the work undertaken by these researchers in controlling the characteristics and life cycle of the apple tree. Some of it appears to show the worst aspects of modern science, in its violent, reductionist methods and its tendency to reshape nature to fit capitalist societies" needs. The fact that the apple tree can be transformed from a beautiful 20–30 foot tree to an eight-foot stick with no branches, stuck in a pot, was finally too outrageous for it to be allowed to pass without comment.

The gaps that have appeared are in the section on Commodification of Symbolism, in which no texts could be found. Also on the work of the orchard worker, who seems to be totally ignored along with the many other horticultural workers. Even Howard Newby who is one of the few writers to broach the subject of agricultural workers" conditions has neglected horticultural workers and this remains something that should be rectified.

after thought, action

DOWN WITH EMPIRE! UP WITH SPRING!
Do or Die Issue Ten

An Insurgency of Dreams

Defend the Collective Imagination. Beneath the cobblestones, the beach
~*Slogan daubed in Paris, May 1968*

The radical ecological movement was born from the worldwide revolutionary upsurge of the 1960s and '70s. Love of the Earth and for each other has always been with us, but in that period these feelings exploded across the world in a way they hadn't for decades. In nearly every land people came together and resisted. In some areas there were decisive victories for people in the battle against power; in others, power won hands down.

The epic struggle of the Vietnamese people and the anti-Vietnam war actions across the world; urban guerrillas across Europe; barricades in Paris; the European squatting movement, the brutal end of the Prague Spring; the rise of the Black Power movement.

This upsurge brought with it the (re)birth of the feminist, ecological, indigenous and libertarian ideas that now form the basis of our worldview.

Authoritarian Communism had dominated the radical movements ever since the Bolshevik counter-revolution. After having been physically exterminated in country after country, anarchist/libertarian groups started once again to grow. Industrial development accelerated in the "Third World" following World War Two. The global elite extended its tentacles, attempting to assimilate or exterminate tribes and band societies outside its control. In turn "indigenous" peoples fought back. In the 1970s the American Indian Movement (AIM) re-launched indigenous armed resistance in North America, reminding us that even the capitalist core countries were always colonies.

Seeing the horrors inflicted on our imprisoned non-human relations — in laboratories, abattoirs and factory farms — the animal liberation movement was born with sabotage at its centre. New generations took up the standard of women's liberation, challenging not only the dominant society but also its patriarchal (loyal) opposition that forever sidelined women's lives in the cause of the (male) workers struggle.

After decades of almost universal techno-worship, not least by radicals, many people began to see that the earth was being destroyed, and started trying both to defend it and regain understanding.

The Rise of Environmentalism

It's time for a warrior society to rise up out of the Earth and throw itself in front of the juggernaut of destruction.
~*Dave Foreman, US EF! co-founder*

The Western environmental movement grew as part of the upsurge, but also in large part as a postscript. When the barricades — both actual and metaphorical — were cleared, a generation of Western radicals looked to new fronts while many others retreated to rural idylls and communes. What they both found was strength in nature and a burning urge to defend it. This early environmental movement fundamentally challenged the established conservation organisations which for so long had acted as mere (ineffective) park keepers.

At sea a raw energy propelled tiny dinghies to confront the nuclear and whaling industries. On land new organisations were forming, fighting toxic waste dumps, logging, mining and other essentials of industry. Scientists were uncovering huge cataclysms facing the earth and — to elite horror — breaking ranks. This environmentalism had a threatening potential that had to be defused — an army of hacks, cops, advertisers and ideologues got to work.

Capital and state both attacked environmentalists while simultaneously funding counter-tendencies to steer the movement away from confrontation and towards co-operation. This carrot and stick approach co-opted many; groups which had looked promising succumbed to respectability and corporate funding. Environmentalists were given a seat at the table but the talk was not of nature but of compromise, techno-fix and corporate greenwash. Assimilation.

In fact, as early as 1972, The Ecologist magazine (at the time printing articles on the links between ecology and anarchy) carried an editorial entitled 'Down with Environmentalism' saying: "We must repudiate the term environmental. It is too far gone to be rescued."[1]

All through the '70s environmental groups were gaining increased support and membership lists were expanding dramatically. By building mass based organisations environmentalism was split into campaigners and supporters. Bigger offices and bigger salaries were needed to manage the movement. This division — a creation of scale — acted (and still acts) as a terrible internal pressure crushing the radical content and practical usefulness of groups.

Those attracted to 'campaign' jobs were often exactly the wrong class of people (inclined to paper pushing rather than physical action) while most of the support their 'supporters' gave was the annual return of cheques and membership forms — conscience-salving exercises. When serious people got involved in groups their action was often curtailed by other 'campaigners' (or the cop in their own head) reminding them that it could alienate the 'public' and thus cut into membership and funding.

This process was as prevalent in what was then the most radical of the environmental groups — Greenpeace (GP). In 1977 Paul Watson one of GPs directors (who became an icon when he drove a dinghy straight into the path of a whaling harpoon) was heading an expedition to the Newfoundland ice floes. At one point he grabbed a club used to kill baby harp seals and threw it into the waters. The sealers dunked and nearly drowned him yet worse was to come on return to the office — betrayal. Throwing the club into the sea was criminal damage and he was told by a faceless lawyer, "I don't think you understand what Greenpeace is all about." He was expelled from the corporation.

Watson went on to found the whaler-sinking Sea Shepherd (more of them later) while Greenpeace just got bigger, gaining millions of members while all the time becoming more symbolic and less of a threat. As GP's founder Bob Hunter said with an air of depression. "Nothing could be done to stop it from growing. It'll keep growing and growing, a juggernaut that is out of control."[2]

Meanwhile the global attack on the wild was left largely unabated. Christopher Maines in Green Rage put it well:

"Like the Youth movement, the women's movement, and rock and roll, the reform environmental movement suffered from its own success. It entered the '70s as a vague critic of our society and exited as an institution, wrapped in the consumerism and political ambitions it once condemned. In their drive to win credibility with the government agencies and corporations... the new professional environmentalists seemed to have wandered into the ambiguous world of George Orwell's Animal Farm, where it was increasingly difficult to tell the farmers from the pigs."[3]

The Birth of Earth First!

So, from the vast sea of raging moderation, irresponsible compromise, knee-jerk rhetorical Sierra Club dogma, and unknowing (OK, sometimes knowing) duplicity in the systematic destruction of the earth, a small seed of sanity sprouts: Earth First!

Howie Wolke, EF! co-founder.

In 1980 five friends hiked into the desert. All long term activists sick with careerism, legality and failure, they knew a new kind of group was needed. One that would break the law, push open the envelope, hit the corporations where it hurt (in the pocket) and most of all never EVER compromise in defence of mother earth. Around their camp fire Earth First! was born.

EF!s first act was one of sarcastic symbolism — and defection. In a land full of memorials to the genocidal victor, EF! raised a plaque commemorating Victorio, an Apache who wiped out a mining camp.

"Victorio, Outstanding Preservationist and Great American. This monument celebrates the 100th Anniversary of the great Apache chief, Victorio's, raid on the Cooney mining camp near Mogollon, New Mexico, on April 28th, 1880. Victorio strove to protect these mountains from mining and other destructive activities of the white race. The present Gila Wilderness is partly a fruit of his efforts. Erected by the New Mexico Patriotic Heritage Society"

The next action EF! pulled off was at the Glen Canyon Dam, where a three hundred foot polythene banner was unfurled down the side of the dam, looking for all the world like a vast crack opening up. The demonstrators chanted RAZE THE DAM. People had campaigned in the past against new dams but no one had ever had the audacity to campaign to pull down those already built. The Glen Canyon Dam in fact held special significance. In a sickening deal the big environmental groups had accepted the damming of the canyon in return for the cancellation of a dam elsewhere. This was exactly the kind of compromise EF! was founded to resist.

Thus from the very beginning EF!ers set themselves not only the task of defending the last fragments but of reversing the process: pulling down the dams and the powerlines. EF! launched its proposal for a network of vast wilderness preserves — half of Nevada for instance would be declared "off limits to industrial human civilisation, as preserves for the free flow of natural processes."

EF! didn't want people to wait for the state to set them up. Instead the people themselves should make them happen — direct action. If logging needed stopping — stop it, blockade it, trash the machines. If a road needed digging up — DIG IT UP! This militancy was a touchstone of even early EF!, but it wasn't just its militancy that made it stand out globally (though it shocked Americans). All around the world groups were turning to direct action in environmental struggles. In both Britain and Germany, for example, anti-nuclear mass action had been growing apace. What was really unique in the environmental movement was EF!s militant biocentrism.

The wilderness proposals preamble stated: "the central idea of EF! is that humans have no divine right to subdue the Earth, that we are merely one of several million forms of life on this planet. We reject even the notion of benevolent stewardship as that implies dominance. Instead we believe that we should be plain citizens of the Land community."

Echoing *The Ecologist*'s earlier denunciation of environmentalism Dave Foreman goes one step further.

"Wilderness is the essence of everything we're after. We aren't an environmental group. Environmental groups worry about environmental health hazards to human beings, they worry about clean air and water for the benefit of people and ask us why we're so wrapped up in something as irrelevant and tangential and elitist as wilderness. Well, I can tell you a wolf or a redwood or a grizzly bear doesn't think wilderness is elitist. Wilderness is the essence of everything. It's the real world."[4]

Within a year EF! moved beyond symbolism to direct struggle. Around the country a combination of civil disobedience and sabotage halted logging and oil drilling. Groups were setting up all over. What many in industry had originally written off as a joke was quickly becoming a nightmare. In 1985 EF!ers published *Ecodefence: A Field Guide to Monkeywrenching*. This was unashamed, heads held high 350-page manual on how to trash pretty much any machine with which civilisation attacks the wild. Written by over 100 contributors to the *Earth First! Journal*, this book was information for action.

Diggers trashed, forests occupied, billboards subverted, logging roads dug up, trees spiked, offices invaded, windows smashed, snares disabled, computers scrapped — EF! was on the move.

But so now was the State.

The FBI wasn't about to let a crew of hippies, feminists, cowboys and desert anarchists continue to hammer company profits. The late '80s onwards saw a wave of reaction that included infiltration, set ups, conspiracy trials, raids, corporate directed anti-environmental hate groups and even assassination attempts on "leading" EF!ers. This was a continuation of the FBI's COINTELPRO (Counter Insurgency Programme) previously unleashed in the '60s/'70s upsurge against the Weather Underground, the New Left, the American Indian Movement, the Black Panthers and the Puertorican liberation movement. Now some of the same agents that had destroyed those movements were overseeing the attack on EF!

Pre-existing divisions over philosophy, tactics and not least of all personality were exacerbated by the crisis that engulfed EF! A split begun to emerge between supporters of EF! co-founder Dave Foreman and long term California organiser Judi Bari. All the while both were under serious corporate/state attack. Foreman was woken up one morning with an FBI gun to his head and charged with conspiracy to down power lines. Bari was carbombed.

The split and state attacks seriously weakened US EF! and it would never fully recover it's accelerating drive. Nevertheless survive it did and at the beginning of the '90s it was still the kickass environmental movement of the developed world. It's actions, ideas and attitude would inspire a massive wave of action across the Atlantic.

Corporate/state repression of EF! led to its logical conclusion with the car bombing of California EF! activists Judi Bari and Daryll Cherney. They were targeted during the successful Redwood Summer forest blockades. The bomb exploded directly below Judi, who awoke in hospital with major injuries. The police then attempted to frame her for her own bombing. Judi is now dead, but her estate has continued to drag the FBI through the courts.

EF! Crosses the Atlantic

The climate in Britain in 1991 was similar to that which had given birth to US EF! Organisations that had started off quite radical in the '70s were well and truly assimilated. Big offices, good salaries, lobbying and little else.

Back in 1972, in its first ever newsletter, FoE UK stated: "We want to avoid the centre-periphery situation, whereby an organisation's forces and resources tend to be drawn to the centre, to 'head office' while patently the strength of the group... is derived from experience in the field."[5]

By the '90s FoE had undeniably failed to avoid the 'centre-periphery situation' (to put it politely). Greenpeace was even more centrist — its local groups simply fundraisers.[6] The late '80s had seen a massive increase in support for environmental groups yet nothing real was happening. Something more radical — and practical — was needed.

On the south coast in the seedy kiss-me-quick seaside town of Hastings some sixth form students were plotting. They were bored out of their minds by A-levels and disillusioned with FoE. In contrast the biocentric approach of US EF! and its victorious direct action tactics were inspiring. The wild was calling...

They formed Britain's first EF! group with a handful of people and no resources. Within a few months they would be making headlines — for now they spray painted Hastings. A year later they had kick-started the biggest wave of ecological defence Britain has seen since the vanquishing of the peasantry. [7] So as to cover the last decade relatively briefly I'm going to have to paint with big strokes. The time covered divides (pretty) neatly into three overlapping stages:

Earth First! Birth Period (1991-1993)
Land Struggle Period (1993 — 1998)
Consolidation and Global Resistance Period (1998 — 2002)

EF! Birth Period (1991-1993)

Earth First! hit the headlines when two EF!ers flew from Britain to the rainforests of Sarawak. At the time the Penan tribes were barricading logging roads and standing up to the corporate attack on their home — the forest. The two joined the blockades and for their efforts were locked up for two months in a stinking Malay jail. This news story went through the roof — much to the annoyance of both the Malaysian government and the UK's leading environmental groups.

FoE Central Office publicly denounced EF!, arguing that by taking action in Sarawak the EF!ers AIDED the Malaysian government who wanted to paint all opposition as emanating from the West. This position ignored that the Penan had requested that people join them and that the Malaysian government was unlikely to halt the destruction without increased PHYSICAL opposition. As one of the imprisoned EF!ers said: "In our absence from Britain we had been tried and convicted by the mainstream groups. They have convicted us of a crime they themselves could never be accused of: action. With friends like these, the Earth doesn't need enemies."

This was the first of many public attacks on the new generation of radical ecological activists by the headquarters of the environmental NGOs. The difference between the two tendencies was shown in July 1991. While the Sarawak Two were in prison the annual meeting of the G7 (worlds seven leading state powers) came to London. EF!ers with no money and few numbers carried out a number of actions — banner drops outside and disruption of meetings inside. The NGOs submitted reports. This mobilisation by EF! was small but a portent of things to come. The next time the G7 came to Britain the radical ecological movement would field not dozens but thousands...

Thanks to the Sarawak campaign the Hastings lot quickly began to make links with people around the country from a variety of pre-existing networks: Green Anarchist, the (embryonic) Rainforest Action Network, ALF, Green Student groups, peace groups, local FoE and the hunt saboteurs. Out of a generation largely consisting of students and doleys disillusioned with mainstream environmentalism, groups sprang up in London, Brighton, Glastonbury, Liverpool, Oxford, Manchester and Norwich.

Inspired by abroad the handful of new activists went about importing the North American/Australian model. What this meant was a combination of non-violent civil disobedience, media stunts, and monkey-wrenching. Actions were organised as part of international rainforest days co-ordinated in the US and Australia. Australia had seen some recent big dock blockades and the tactic was quickly brought to Britain.

On December 4th 1991, in what was EF!'s first really successful action, 200 people invaded Tilbury docks in London. That month the EF! Action Update also reported under the headline 'Reclaim the Streets' — A small roadblock done by South Downs EF! More was to be heard of Reclaim the Streets ...

Tilbury was followed by a 400-strong protest at Liverpool docks.

> On the first day we stormed the fences, occupied cranes, piles of dead rainforest, observation towers and machinery; we hung banners off everything and blocked the busy dock road... Police relations were good; because of full liaison work, violence on both sides was prevented and we all got on like good mates. This was helped with good legal backup, and non-violence training from experienced CND activists... People stayed up the cranes all night ... The second day saw a complete change in attitude by the authorities. They'd let us have our fun on the first day and they were determined that the ship would dock on the Wednesday. Under fear of violence, our press office got the media straight down there — our strongest weapon against foul play, but already the police were wading in and holding people in a big cage.[10]

The description of State force as "foul play" and our greatest protection from it being the media illustrates well the startlingly naive views held by many at the time. The dock-workers refused to unload the shipment while EF!ers were still running around in danger. Eventually the police cleared the dock and the shipment was unloaded.

February saw the first anti-road direct action at Twyford Down. FoE held a symbolic chaining up of the site which they ended when injuncted. At the request of the Twyford Down Association EF!ers from all over the country started a wave of site actions, sabotage and blockades. Offices started to be targeted around this time with an example being the chaining up of the Malaysian airline office by 29 activists in solidarity with 31 Penan on trial.[11]

While the national days of actions at Twyford continued down south, up north the campaign to stop peat extraction from Thorne Moors hotted up. On Monday April 13th £100,000 of damage was done to Fisons machinery. A telephone call to the media claimed the action for Earth First! FoE central office quickly condemned the action on television.

In many ways the first few months of 1992 set a pattern of activism prevalent for much of the next decade — a cycle of national actions, anti-road campaigns, office occupations, night-time sabotage and street blockades. The South Downs hosted Britains first EF! gathering in April 1992.

Around 60 people turned up to discuss direction, aims and plan future actions. While EF! was quite unified at the time, divisions were definitely present. The recent Moors sabotage and unwise interviews to the press concerning the future environmental use of explosives caused quite a stir. Most agreed that if EF! itself was seen to do criminal damage then it would put groups at risk. A line of 'We neither condemn nor condone' was agreed upon.

For some this was simply a legal technicality — in reality EF!ers would still be doing damage. For the less militant faction it was seen as meaning civil disobedience was the tactic for EF! while sabotage was secondary, separate and something done by others. Though I'd still say that the wet faction was wrong, it was understandable given the widespread paranoia following the then recent Arizona conspiracy trial and the FBI bombing of EF!ers.

In this period EF! was primarily involved nationally in two campaigns: rainforests and anti-roads. While similar tactics were used for both they had fundamentally different characters. While rainforest days of action would trail off, anti-road action would get bigger and bigger. While the rainforest actions were often very successful — on their own terms — they rarely lasted more than a day. On May 11th '92 over 100 invaded the yard of Britain's biggest mahogany importer. Though a successful action in itself, it remained in the whole a media stunt. The site remained operative, the offices weren't trashed and next day it opened up again as usual. We all felt empowered by the action, but there was a different feeling at Twyford Down. At Twyford the movement could engage in protracted physical resistance. It was a land struggle. You could feel the land you were struggling over with your hands and your soul. When people started to move onto the land itself they connected with it, became part of it. Standing in the sun, grass between your toes looking to the diggers on the horizon the rage grew. It wasn't a single issue — it was war.

On an entirely practical level it was a focus; an easily accessible battleground local groups could drive their vans to. In this struggle EF! grew and evolved. Most actions through '92 were done by between 10-50 people and commonly resulted in minor arrests for breach of the peace. Sabotage commenced almost immediately. The site was regularly flooded by redirecting the River Itchens water and machines were wrenched.

Just as it was new for us so too it was for the state, who were surprisingly unprepared. In these first few months it would be case of running onto site, climbing a crane or locking onto a digger. An hour or so later the state's most regular foot-soldier would arrive — Bill Aud, a copper with a sideline in mobile disco.

The Camps Begin...

The need for groups to have somewhere to sleep after travelling distances for days of action was the catalyst that set up Britains first ever ecological direct action camp. A traveller site had long graced one side of the hill, but in June an obviously separate action camp was set up on the dongas — an area of threatened downland furrowed deep with sheep droves. This became a base for action against the road-building that was going on further down the hill. On the dongas a real feeling of tribe developed as many more were attracted to the site by summer beauty and direct action.

While some travellers had early on got involved in EF!,[12] it was at Twyford that a real mix started to develop between (predominately urban) EF!/Animal lib types and (predominately rural) travellers. Each threw different ingredients into the campfire cauldron (of veggie slop). The activists — action techniques. The Travellers — on the land living skills. Teepees and benders sprung up, machines were trashed. This crossover would propel ecological direct action into a potent cycle of struggle with big numbers and big successes.

However while both sides complimented each other it would be ridiculous to iron over the very real family squabbles. As the summer progressed there was tension within the Dongas Tribe over what offensive actions should be taken and what defensive measures should be put in place. Discussion of how to resist the (obviously imminent) eviction was silenced with the classic hippy refrain: 'If you think negative things, negative things will happen." It was even suggested, in a basically religious formulation, that mother earth would simply not 'allow' the destruction of the dongas to happen. This tendency grew as the months went on until by autumn serious conflict reared up. Following a threat by security to repeat an earlier arson attack on the camp in retaliation for site sabotage, offensive action was actually "banned" by a "meeting of the tribe." Hippie authoritarian pacifists[13] practically "banished" EF!ers who had been involved from the start. Predictably, however, the State wasn't standing idle — it was preparing.

Elsewhere the campaign against roads was building apace. New road openings were disrupted and the newspapers were already talking about the 'next Twyford' — the battle for Oxleas Wood in London. Across the country the government boasted it was building the biggest road programme since the Romans. These roads smashed through some of the most biologically important areas — SSSIs (Special Sites of Scientific Interest) and so it was obvious that by fighting roads one could take on Thatchers "Great Car Economy," while directly defending important habitat. Direct action was starting to spread beyond roads. At Golden Hill in Bristol an impressive community resistance against Tesco destroying local green space resulted in arrests and mass policing. A new air was definitely abroad.

Back at Twyford the inevitable eviction came brutally on December 9th — Yellow Wednesday. A hundred Group 4 security guards escorted bulldozers in to trash the camp. Throwing themselves in front of the landrovers and machines those in the camp slowed the eviction — suffering arrests and injuries. Two were rendered unconscious by cops; lines of coiled razor wire crossed the down. The drama appearing live on television brought local ramblers, environmentalists, kids and the simply shocked to the site, many of whom without hesitation joined the resistance. Others came from around the country, making the eviction last three days. The eviction was an important moment — deeply depressing to most involved, it nevertheless captured the imagination of thousands.

> Many, particularly the media, who like a nice neat story — will see the move of the Dongas Camp as the closing act of the Twyford drama, but the battle has not ended — it's beginning. If they think they can stop us with threats and violence, we've got to make damn sure they don't. Hunt sabs regularly get hassle but carry on regardless — let's learn from their example. Obstruction on site needs to be co-ordinated and supported. The number of days work lost is what counts. To broaden it out nationally, every Tarmac and associated subcontractors office, depots and sites in the country should be targeted. Every leaflet produced should contain the information needed for a cell to wreak £10,000 of havoc against the contractors and even put smaller sub-contractors out of business. No Compromise in Defence of Planet Earth!
>
> *— Do or Die* No.1, Jan 1993

From the Ashes... Twyford Rising!

In February following an eventful invasion of Whatley Quarry, a new camp was set up at Twyford. Off route and up on the hill overlooking the cutting, this camp, and those that followed it, would have a very different attitude than the one on the dongas. Not defence, ATTACK! Starting with half a dozen campers (Camelot EF!) the site steadily grew through spring with direct action practically everyday — and many nights too! Some actions were carried out by a handful of people locking onto machines, others were mass invasions by hundreds. Diggers were trashed, offices invaded. A sunrise circle-dance was followed by an eight car sabotage convoy.

The State response to these actions grew more organised: hordes of guards, private investigators and cops were stationed daily to stop the actions.

They failed. Endless arrests, restrictive bail conditions, camp evictions and harassment only hardened resolve. By late April the Department of Transport was in the High Court pushing for an injunction on 76 named individuals. To back up their case they produced evidence nearly a foot thick with hilarious daily reports from Twyford. A not unusual entry read thus:

> At 0845hrs a group of protestors raided one of the small earthmoving operations at Shawford Down and did some very severe damage to the excavator before making off. There were between 35-50 of them and they seemed to know exactly what to do to cause the most damage to the machines.[14]

Unsurprisingly the High Court backed the DoT and injuncted the 76. The reaction from our side was swift, two days after the hearing 500 joined a Mass Trespass at the cutting. In a moving sign of multi-generational resistance the crowd was addressed by Benny Rothman, one of the leaders of the 1932 Kinder Scout Trespass. The mass injunction breaking resulted in six being sent to jail for a month — the first of many to end up in the clink for fighting road building. On the day of their release they were greeted by friends, smiles, hugs and... sabotage. In Collingham, Linconshire, under the spray painted title "For the Prisoners of Twyford Down," the following was wrenched: Three bulldozers, three Tarmac Trucks, two Diesel Pumps, a Work Shed and a Control Station.[15]

Tarmac PLC was feeling the pressure. Across the country many of its offices were occupied, its machines targeted. When its AGM was disrupted the directors made their fears known. Thanks to good corporate research their home addresses had been uncovered and published. Some had been freaked enough to hire security guards — their apprehension heightened by past targeting of directors by Animal Liberationists. Considering the relatively few "radical eco" home visits since, this may seem surprising. However at this time the movement was influenced by quite divergent groups. The fact that directors were largely left unscathed in the years to come was not a given — it was a choice.

During that summer everything from druid curses to burning tarmac was hurled at the contractors in a hectic campaign which was; "a symbol of resistance, a training ground, a life changer and a kick up the arse to the British green movement."[16] Nevertheless, though it slowed it, the M3 was not stopped. "The cutting at Twyford Down gets ever deeper and the down, the water-meadows and of course most of the dongas are now destroyed, but it's destruction has given birth to a movement and the fight goes on."[17]

As the resistance at Twyford waned anti-road actions were spreading across the country like wildfire. Digger diving was organised on a near-daily basis at Wymondham near Norwich, and in Newcastle hammocks were strewn in the trees at Jesmond Dene. Like Twyford, once again it was local EF!ers and residents that catalysed the intial actions that burgenoned into widescale tribal resistance on the land.

Further north, action was hotting up in Scotland with tree and crane sits, some lasting days, connected to the M74 in Glasgow. Even further north was the campaign against the Skye Bridge, a monstrosity cutting across the Kyle of Lockash, immortalised in the environmental classic, *The Ring of Bright Water*. The bridge not only affected the direct habitat (famous for its otters) but connected the Hebrides into the mainland infrastructure, endangering the whole regions ecology by exposing it to further development.

Unfortunately at the time there was only limited active local support for resistance. The first and only day of action against the building was carried out by around a dozen, who, bar a few from Skye and Glasgow EF!, were all from "south of the border." As cops stationed on the island could be counted on one hand, reinforcements were brought in. Inflatables were launched as the main work was being carried out off barges. The reaction of the construction firm was brutal — industrial hoses were used as water-cannons in an attempt to knock those up floating cranes into the sea. The Scottish press were present in numbers and also enjoyed some corporate PR. The front page of *The Scotsman* put it like this: "Journalistic objectivity is a wonderful thing. However, it is easily damaged, especially by people trying to ram your boat, sink you, throw rocks at you, then threatening you first with a crowbar and then a grappling hook, not to mention attacking you with a tracked excavator."[18]

The boats were impounded and most were arrested. Bussed a hundred miles away, the group was given strict bail by an all-powerful "Roving Sheriff" (another great colonial legacy) not to return to the Highlands and Islands for over a year. Police escorted the van most of the way to the border. Elsewhere actions were taken against the projects funders, The Bank of America, but the campaign was effectively stillborn by low local involvement and immediate corporate/state "direct action."

A very different situation had produced a very different result at Oxleas Wood in London. These woods in SE London were widely believed to be the next big battle and 3,000 people had signed a pledge to "Beat the Bulldozers." After over a year of direct action at Twyford and with resistance spreading the government knew it couldn't risk hitting such a beautiful place within "recruitment distance" of millions. The summer of 1993 saw this £300 million scheme dropped, a major victory after just a year of sustained action against infrastructural growth.

Not Single Issues, Just One War

This success was all the more impressive considering that this campaign, though then becoming the dominant terrain of struggle for the movement, was still only one of the battles it was involved in. The daily fight on the land was interspersed with national and local days of action across the country on a range of issues.

Timber depots in Oxford, Rochdale and London were all targeted by days of action. One national week of action against mahogany saw "ethical shoplifting" (the seizure of illegally logged timber from shops), in towns across the country; and abroad the simultaneous total destruction of logging equipment by the Amazonian Parkana Indians![19] Other actions included bank occupations (against Third World debt), an ICI factory invasion (to highlight continued ozone depletion), road blockades (against car culture) and regular quarry blockades at Whatley in Somerset. These different battles were all viewed as part of the same war by EF!ers. Many of the hundreds that invaded Oxford Timbnet for the second time had come direct from a weekend of action at Twyford. The next day a cavalcade moved onto Bristol to help disrupt the opening of the disputed Golden Hill Tesco. Then, as now (maybe more so) many EF!ers were also involved in the animal liberation movement. The campaigns were carried out in a global context of escalating radical ecological resistance. Anti-road campaigns in the (French) Pyranees, anti-whaling action by Sea Shepherd (around Norway), the campaign against the Narmada Dam (in India), the Ogoni struggle against Shell (Nigeria), EF! defence of the Danube (in Slovakia), biotech companies bombed (in Switzerland), GM crop experiments dug up (in the Netherlands), and of course anti-logging battles (in North America, the Pacific, the Amazon and Australia).

It's a long way from North America to Newcastle but in 1993 the tactic of protracted tree-sits crossed the Atlantic. Following demos earlier in the year the bulldozers had gone into Jesmond Dene unannounced on June 16th. The State, however, hadn't factored in skiving Geordie kids, who stopped the machines working while the alarm went out. The next morning protestors barricaded the site entrance. More kids came back and shovelled earth with plastic flowerpots to build up the barricade — the Flowerpot Tribe was born. The campfire was set burning and a strong community formed. A combination of "local talent" and reinforcements from Twyford and elsewhere, made the next five months an avalanche of site occupations, tree-sitting, piss-taking and nightly sabotage. The legendary winds of Newcastle seemed to blow down the construction site fencing again and again! The kids sang: "The Chainsaws, the Chainsaws — they cut down all out trees. The Pixies, the Pixies, trashed their JCBs." Of course despite the laughs it was hard.

Everyone is getting very knackered and pissed off — tree sitting is saving the trees that are hammocked, but it's tiring, cold, stressful and often boring. Ground support people face prison for breaking injunctions as they take food to trees. It's GRIM for sitters when the trees are felled near them. Local people sab a cement mixer under the copper beech by throwing rock salt into it — a workman goes berserk and tries attacking the beech with a JCB, trying to knock the tree-sitters out. He survived but the copper beech loses another couple of branches.[20]

In 1991 EF!'s handful of activists were the radical ecological movement. By the end of the summer of 1993, EF! not only had 45 local groups but had catalysed thousands to take direct action — mostly not under the EF! banner. Now one could really begin to talk about a movement. After the Jesmond Dene camps were evicted one of the Flowerpot Tribe wrote: "Those who've been involved are also gearing up to fight other schemes... What we've learnt will spread out to other road and environmental protests... it just gets bigger and bigger. If we can't stop the bastards totally we can COST them, show them there's no easy profit in Earth rape. They've already been cost millions — let's cost them some more."[21]

Land Struggle Period (1993 — 1998)

Land struggles were infectious, the next period seeing an explosion of activity. The winning combination was relatively solid networks of long term anti-road campaigners (ALARM UK), a nationwide network of EF! groups and most importantly a swelling "tribe" willing to travel across the land.

While the State had backed down at Oxleas it intended to go full steam ahead with the M11 link through East London. DoT bureaucrats and politicians probably thought the movement wouldn't pull together over the destruction of a small amount of trees and hundreds of working class homes. They were wrong. Hundreds of the houses were already squatted, long since having been compulsorily purchased. This vibrant scene was joined by others from Jesmond and Twyford. With much of the road smashing through a long-term squatting community and a solidly working class area, this more than any previous anti-road campaign was a defence of human lives as well as wildlife. Nevertheless, there were beautiful patches of overgrown gardens and copses, and the struggle was also understood in the national ecological context.

By halting the road in London we can save woodlands, rivers and heathlands all the way to Scotland, without endangering their ecology by having mud fights with hundreds of security guards and police in their midst.[22]

The first real flashpoint came at a chestnut tree on George Green, common land in the heart of Wanstead. The 10ft hoardings which had been erected to enclose the common were trashed by a jolly mob of kids, activists and local people. On the Green a hunched woman in her 80s was crying. She had always felt powerless, but when she pushed the fences down with hundreds of others, she said she felt powerful for the first time in her life. Empowerment is direct action's magic, and the spell was spreading.

> A treehouse was built in the branches of the chestnut tree... For the following month the campfire became a focal point... People from different backgrounds began to get to know one another, spending long evenings together, talking, forming new friendships. Something new and beautiful had been created in the community. Many local people talk of their lives having been completely changed by the experience.[23]

The eviction came in December and was carried out by 400 police. With 150 people resisting it took nine hours to bring down one tree! Sabotage also played a part — both of the contractor's hydraulic platforms had been wrenched the night before.

> The eviction had forced the DoT to humiliate itself in a very public way. The loss of the tree was a tragic day, and yet also a truly wonderful day. It had hammered another huge nail in the coffin of the roads programme.[24]

The State hoped this was the end of No M11, but it was just the beginning. Other areas had already been occupied, and regular action against the contractors continued. It was a fitting end to the second year of concerted action against roads. On January 1st 1994 the Indigenous Zapatistas of Mexico launched themselves on to the stage of world history. Liberating town after town, freeing prisoners, re-distributing food, declaring themselves autonomous of the new economic order.

They didn't just redistribute food; they redistributed hope worldwide, and were to have a significant impact on the movement here. Meanwhile in Britain the year nearly started off with a big bang. In January a very small amount of broadsheet coverage reported the police detonation of an explosive device under the main bridge at Twyford Down. Coverage also reported a bomb found at Tarmac's HQ.[25]

The Spring saw camps sprout up against the Wymondham Bypass near Norwich, the Leadenham Bypass in Lincolnshire, the Batheastern-Swainswick Bypasses outside Bath and the Blackburn Bypass in Lancashire.

In inner-city Manchester, a threatened local park got a dose of eco-action at Abbey Pond. Back in the East End, Spring saw vast defensive and offensive road-resisting. A row of large Edwardian houses were next en route — they were barricaded, and Wanstonia was born: "it was declared an autonomous free zone.

People made joke passports and the like. We were digging this huge trench all the way around the site. Doing that probably had zero tactical effectiveness but it really made us feel that this was where the UK ended and our space started."[26] The State does not take well to losing territory.

> In a scene reminiscent of a medieval siege, around 800 police and bailiffs supported by cherry-pickers and diggers besieged the independent state of Wanstonia. After cordoning off the area the invaders preceded to storm the five houses. The police had to break through the barricades to enter only to find the staircases removed thus forcing them to get in through roofs or upper floors. Some protestors were on the roofs having chained themselves to the chimneys, the contractors preceded to destroy the houses while many people were still occupying them… It took ten hours to remove 300 people.[27]

This impressive and costly eviction was followed up by Operation Roadblock — a month of rota-based daily direct action, where groups booked in which days they would take action. It worked remarkably well, with sizeable disruption every day through March. Elsewhere many of the resistance techniques developed at the M11, both for the defence of houses and trees, were now being used against other schemes.

Progress, Yuck — Time to Go Back to the Trees

Tactics were evolving fast. At Jesmond, temporary hammocks had graced the branches; at George Green a single treehouse had been built; at Bath the first real network of treehouses hit the skyline; in Blackburn there was a full-on Ewok-style Tree Village. Unable to defeat the bailiffs on the ground, resistance had moved skyward.

"You'd be standing at the fire at night, and it would be the first time you'd been down on the ground all day. You'd look up and there would be all these little twinkles from candles up above you… How were they going to get us out?… I don't think I can describe here how special it is to sleep and wake in the branches of a tree. To see the stars and the moon. To feel the sunshine and feel the rain."[28]

Hundreds were now living on-site across the country, with many, many more "weekending" or visiting for days of action. Most campaigns were now setting up multiple camps, each taking a slightly different form according to the lay of the land. Previously, barricades had been built around houses and woodlands — now they themselves were transformed into barricades — complex networks of walkways, treehouses, lock-ons, concrete and determination.

Solsbury Hill's fourth site eviction at Whitecroft was the first full-on, all-treetop eviction. Using cherry-pickers and standard chainsaw men, the Sheriff failed to take down a single tree; the camp had defeated him... for now. The cost was high; one protestor hospitalised with spinal injuries and a collapsed lung. Ten days later the Sheriff returned, this time with madder baliffs — Equity card-holding stunt men. These were more crazy, muscular and willing to take risks with their own lives as well as of those in the trees. By the end of the day Whitecroft was no more. This — the most spectacular at the time — was only one of the many conflicts countrywide. These evictions were becoming hugely costly — to the contractors, to the state, and to social stability. Most sites at this time continued offensive action as well, using the by then standard formula; digger diving, office occupations and crane-sits, alongside overt and covert sabotage. The state was being challenged — it would soon escalate its response.

With every campaign the movement seemed to be going from strength to strength, with one exception, Leadenham. A camp had set up, and the DoT said it was putting the scheme into review, but victory was not to be. The contractors launched a surprise attack — during the "reprieve" — while those still on site were "dealt with" a few weeks later by local thugs. Vigilante attacks on sites had always been an occasional occurrence, but they were usually minor in scale. At Leadenham though there was a sizeable group of pro-road locals willing to take direct action.

> The attack happened following a demo by local people in favour of the bypass. Leadenham villagers decided in their infinite wisdom that a road was preferable to a 'few trees.' Masked vigilantes arrived at the camp at 5am armed with chainsaws. They proceeded to hack down trees protestors had been sitting in. Anyone getting in their way was punched and violently assaulted.[29]

This basically put an end to site occupation at the scheme, though days of action still followed. What Leadenham showed was the absolute necessity of having significant community support IF a camp was set up. Without it, there was a danger of being sitting/sleeping targets. Thankfully, through this period no other sites were mass attacked by local vigilantes in this way.[30]

While in this article I'll give an overview of this period, from so high up one can't hope to focus on the detail — and it's the detail that counts. The incredible moments, the passion, the exhilaration, the waiting, the amazing people, the occasional twat — the tribe. Not to mention the holy trinity: dogs, mud and cider. On site and in the trees, this feeling of togetherness and otherness grew. Leaving site to get food or giros, the harshness and speed of the industrial world hit you; but by living a daily existence of resistance we were hitting back.

Hunting the Machines

Every month brought news of an increase in sabotage despite minimal coverage in either mainstream or radical press, not least because communiqués were rarely sent. Sabotage largely centred around projects where ongoing daytime campaigns were underway, but some was done in solidarity with campaigns further afield. With so many groups fighting multiple schemes by the same companies actions often ended fulfilling both roles. ARC, for instance, had supplied roadstone to Twyford Down and was trying to expand quarries in North Wales and Somerset.

> After forcing their way into the control room [of ARC Penmaemawr quarry] the intruders smashed a glass partition and then caused £10,000 worth of damage to computer equipment."[31]

The scale of sabotage carried out during the '90s land struggles is often forgotten. Altogether the direct costs of replacement and repair at construction sites must have easily run into the tens of millions. Fantasists may dream that this was the work of highly organised anonymous cells, striking and then disappearing[32], but in truth most trashings were carried out by those camping onsite; either subtley during digger diving, raucously as a mob, or covertly after heavy drinking sessions around the campfire. Basically, whenever it was possible, people fucked shit up. The sensible and commendable desire not to boast has left these actions hidden behind newspaper images of smiling "tree-people." The grins though were often those of mischievous machine wreckers; near campfires no yellow monster was safe from the hunt.

Some celebrity liberals[33] argued "criminal damage" should not have a place in campaigns as it would put off "normal everyday people." This ridiculous idea was even stupider considering one of the main groups consistently carrying out sabotage were those locals with jobs and families who didn't have available (day)time to live on site, and for whom arrests for minor digger-diving could lead to unemployment and family problems.

For many "normal everyday people" covert sabotage was less risky than overt "civil disobedience." Another group of locals that always took to "environmental vandalism' like ducks to water were kids, nearly always the most rebellious section of any community, often with the most intimate relationship to the local environment. Of course despite what I say above, some ecotage was carried out entirely covertly with modus operandi borrowed from the Animal Liberation Front.

> Police believe a £2 million blaze at an Essex construction site could be the work of Green Activists. The fire swept through Cory Environment's aggregates and waste disposal site at Barling, near Southend, ruining four bulldozers, two diggers, and a fleet of six trucks owned by the main contractor. The police say that forensic evidence confirms arson.[34]

There is no Justice, Just Us!

It was becoming obvious that the ecological land struggles were really getting in the way of "progress." The government (correctly) saw the movement as part of a social fabric (travelling culture, festivals, squatting, hunt sabbing) born of the '60s/'70s upsurge. With the Criminal Justice Bill it sought to tear this fabric apart. No more toleration, the government announced; it was giving itself new powers to close free parties, ban demonstrations, create huge exclusion zones, evict squats and jail persistent road-protest "trespassers." Unsurprisingly this challenge was met with a sudden flurry of activity. High street squat info centres around the country; local and national demos. Thousands turned up for marches in London. Rather than deterring people the new laws brought people together — "Unity in Diversity" the call of the day.

On October 9th a demo of 75,000 ended in Hyde Park for the normal ritual of platform speakers. When a sound-system tried to get in at Speakers Corner to turn it into an illegal "party in the park," it was attacked by police. In turn people fought back. The call went out across the Park — Defend the System; thousands ran from the speeches to the action — the Hyde Park Riot had begun.

> Although some people faced up to the police in Park Lane itself, most of the crowd ended up inside the park separated by the metal railings from the riot cops. This made it difficult for the police to launch baton charges or send in the horses, and when they tried to force their way through the small gates in the railings they were repelled with sticks, bottles and whatever was to hand.

There were some very surreal touches while all this was going on: people dancing not far from the police lines, a unicyclist weaving his way through the riot cops, a man fire-breathing. Some people have argued that the police deliberately provoked a riot to make sure the Criminal Justice Bill was passed, but this ignores the fact that there was never any danger of the CJB not being passed, as there had never been any serious opposition within Parliament.[35]

Hyde Park — like the eviction of the Dongas — was a landmark confrontation. At Twyford the movement was forced to face up to the reality of state violence. At Hyde Park it was forced to face the reality of movement violence, the reality being simple — when faced with riot cops many saw nothing wrong with fighting back to defend temporarily liberated space. At the beginning of the march "Keep it Fluffy" stickers had been handed out liberally.

Later as the helicopter floodlights shone down on a riot, the sight of a crusty with a rainbow jumper emblazoned with one of the stickers — throwing a bit of paving slab at the cops — showed how moments of collective power can change people. The following months would see an intensification of "violence/nonviolence" discussions around the country.

When the Bill became an Act in November everyone understood that the only way to defeat a possible 'crackdown' was by defying it. As the EF! Action Update put it: "As far as it affects Earth First!ers... its purpose is not so much to imprison us as to intimidate us — and we mustn't let that work."[36] The day the Act went through on November 4th, activists from No M11 climbed onto the roof of Parliament and unfurled a banner — Defy The Act. Hunt sabs went out in bigger numbers, more road protest camps were established, free parties flourished. By the end of the month a big confrontation came that would test whether the government had succeeded in intimidating the resistance.

A Street Reclaimed

Throughout the Summer, evictions and resistance on the M11 had continued and most of the route was rubble. One major obstacle lay in the path of the bulldozers — Claremont Road, an entire squatted street had been transformed into a surreal otherworld. Turned inside-out, the road itself became the collective living room, the remaining cars flowerbeds. Above the sofa, huge chess board and open fire a vast scaffolding tower reached daily further up to the sky. This "state of the art" reclaimed street was not going to take eviction easy. When it did come, it became the longest and most expensive in English history — five days, 700 police, 200 bailiffs and 400 security guards, costing £2 million.

When the bailiffs arrived they were met by 500 people using every delay tactic possible. A concrete filled car with protruding scaffold poles stopping the cherry pickers moving in. People locked on to the road. Others hung in nets strung across the street. People in bunkers, others huddled on rooftops and in treehouses. Lastly, 12 people scrambled up the 100ft scaffold tower painted with grease and tied with pink ribbons.[37]

One by one, minute by costly minute, the state forces removed the 500 — taking the best part of a week. The sheer ingenuity of the tactics, the resolve of the people involved and the incredible barricading techniques made this an amazing moment. Like the Chestnut Tree, Solsbury Hill and a dozen other evictions, the state won the battle — but they were losing the war. With every hugely expensive eviction, every trashed machine, every delayed contract, every citizen turned subversive, every tree occupied — the social and economic cost of pushing through the roads programme was becoming unbearable.

Yet Claremont — like all anti-roads sites — wasn't simply a reaction to destruction, it was also a reaffirmation of life, of autonomy. It was an experience that changed hundreds of people; its memory would remain precious and propel a whole new wave of streets to be reclaimed. Reclaim the Streets had been formed by EF!ers in '92 to combat the car culture on the city streets.

With the expansion of anti-road resistance the idea had gone into hibernation, but many who had seen the topsy-turvey, inside-out world of Claremont Road wanted to feel the like again. After the end of the M11 campaign, RTS was reformed. The state had foolishly thought Claremont Road lay in rubble; in fact it haunted those who'd been there and its festive rebel spectre would reappear on streets across the country. It started with a reclamation of that bastion of consumption, Camden High Street.

Two cars entered the high street and to the astonishment of passing shoppers ceremoniously piled into each other — crash! Thirty radical pedestrians jumped on top and started trashing them — soon joined by kids. An instant café was set up distributing free food to all and sundry, rainbow carpets unrolled, smothering the tarmac, and a host of alternative street décor... A plethora of entertainment followed including live music, fire-breathing... and the Rinky-Dink bike powered sound system.[38]

A month later and the action was much bigger; word had got around — 1,500 met at the meet-up point, jumped the Tube and arrived at Islington High Street.

They swarmed across the dual carriageway as five 25ft tripods were erected blocking all the access roads. Half a ton of sand was dumped on the tarmac for kids of all ages to build sand castles with. An armoured personnel carrier blasting out rave set up, fire hydrants were opened up — spraying the ravers dancing in the sunshine. All the cops could do was stand to the side and sweat.[39]

While the Claremont eviction was the first major sign of the failure of the CJA, street parties spreading across the country were basically dancing on its grave. With the Act's implementation resistance became a bit more difficult, but its deterrent effect was dead in the water. The rebellion against the CJA had brought together different alternative culture currents and coalesced them into a serious counter-culture; now RTS was making more connections. Above the wonderful spectacle of the Islington Street Party flew a banner declaring solidarity with the Tubeworkers.

Back on the Farm

While London events got the lion's share of media coverage, people were defying the CJA all over, most by simply carrying on with actions — 'business as usual'. The eviction of urban camps at Pollock in Glasgow against the M77 involved hundreds — 250 kids even broke out of school to help stop one eviction. The act had been meant to neuter direct action. Instead in the climate of opposition, whole new struggles opened up, such as those against the live export of sheep and calves, involving thousands more in direct action.

In the south-west the one year anniversary gathering at Solsbury Hill went off with a bang. An Anti-CJA event on the hill ended with lots of fencing pulled down, trashed machinery and security thugs in hospital. As one woman from the local Avon Gorge EF! group put it: "I guess people had had enough of being used as punch bags."[40] This was followed by a day of action with 200 people — stopping most of the work along the route.

Up North the campaign against the M65 saw a major shift in tactics by both those in the trees and those who'd taken the job of getting them out. Three camps had already been evicted, but the crescendo came at Stanworth Valley, an amazing network of walkways, platforms, nets and over 40 treehouses. Through the valley surged the River Ribblesworth. It was truly a village in the sky, which was lucky as the ground was pure quagmire half the time. You've never seen such mud! As well as new people and local activists there was now a dedicated nomadic tribe, seasoned at many previous evictions. After over a year of life in the branches, some were agile and confident at height —

at home in the trees. The state realised that it needed a new force that was as confident on the ropes — Stanworth became the first place where members of the climbing community took sides against nature.

"Upon entering the treetops they were quite shocked to find the people were not just passive spectators to their own removal. A gentle but firm push with the foot often kept them out of a treehouse. Two climbers tried to manhandle an activist out of the trees, mistakenly thinking they were alone. The calls for help were quickly answered and to the climbers' astonishment out of the thick shroud of leaves above, activists abseiled down, others painered up from below and yet more appeared from both sides running along the walkways and branches. The climbers could be forgiven for thinking they were caught in a spider's web."[41]

Eventually after five days, all 120 people had been ripped from the trees — bringing the total contract cost increased by the No M65 campaign to £12.2 million. The climbers had found new lucrative employment but they would do their best to avoid ever repeating an eviction under leaf cover. From now on most evictions would be when the leaves were off the trees; the combined factor of nature's abundance and activist up-for-it attitude a severe deterrent.

The spread of anti-road camps was by now incredible with '95 probably the highpoint in terms of national spread. On top of the established camps, new areas were occupied in Berkshire, Kent, Devon and Somerset. Over the next year the struggle moved well beyond just fighting roads. Camps were set up to protect land from open-cast mining in South Wales, leisure development in Kent and quarrying in the South West. No surprise then that one of the major voices spurring on this "culture of resistance" got some special attention from some special people.

Green Anarchist magazine in the mid '90s was a meeting point of movements. Its readership included significant numbers of travellers, hunt sabs, class struggle anarchos, Green Party members, "eco-warriors," and animal liberationists. It was an obvious target for the secret state. A set of 17 raids aimed at Green Anarchist and the ALF resulted in the jailing of a number of its editors. This repression, like the CJA, backfired. Instead of marginalising GA it actually made them far more well known; an alliance of largely liberal publications swung behind them, motions of support were even brought up at the Green Party and FoE annual conferences. This increased exposure, combined with M15 fears about court documents released in appeal hearings compromising their agents, secured their release. A major aim of the repression against GA had been to deter sabotage, while large parts of the CJA were aimed at stopping "Aggravated Trespass." Their absolute failure to deter the radical ecological direct action movement was shown clearly one morning in Somerset.

Whatley Quarry — Yee Ha!

The "national" EF! action to shut down Whatley Quarry was an even greater success than expected. A week later the owners hadn't managed to restart work. At 5.30am, 400 activists descended on the quarry. Small teams ensured gates were blockaded and all plant and machinery occupied... Detailed maps and a predetermined plan ensured police and security were out manoeuvred. Tripods were carried 9 miles over-night and set up on the quarry's rail line whilst lorries were turned away. Press reports state that £250,000 worth of damage was caused — not counting the cost of a week's lost production, for a quarry normally selling 11,000 tonnes per day! Twenty metres of railway track leading out of the quarry 'disappeared'; the control panel for video monitoring of the plant fell apart; a two storey crane pulled itself to bits; three control rooms dismantled themselves; and several diggers and conveyor belts broke down.[42]

The police managed to arrest 64 people, mostly under the CJA for aggravated trespass. In time, most of the cases were dropped. All through the land struggle period EF! had been organising national actions — this was by far the most effective. It had come on the back of four years of concerted actions at Whatley and showed what can be achieved by good organisation and the element of surprise. While the cops had prepared in their hundreds, they simply hadn't factored in that "hippies" could get up at 4am. This action really set the mood for the next year.

An Adrenaline Junkie's Idea of Heaven

Police on the Newbury Bypass site today condemned the tactics of those who last night took a heavy tractor from road-works and drove to a construction area, where they damaged compound fencing, lighting equipment and a portacabin building. Police were called but the offenders ran away before they arrived at the scene.[43]

The Newbury bypass was the big battle. The scale was immense. Nine miles long, over 30 camps, ten thousand trees, over a thousand arrests. A daily struggle with up to 1,600 security guards[44], hundreds of police, private detectives, and state climbers lined up against tribes of hundreds of committed, mud-living activists. Day after relentless day, evictions and resistance. "Every morning, cider and flies."

I don't have space to cover all the campaigns across the country, so I am focusing on those which saw important changes. Equally, I can't hope to give a true impression of what it was like to be living on site, at Newbury least of all. Crazy and medieval — in both good ways and bad — is all I'll say. (The book Copse captures the spirit of those times best, with a mix of photos, interviews and cartoons. VERY highly recommended!)

The state had by this time learnt from some of its previous mistakes; no longer would it try to clear the road in stages at the same time as building works progressed. In the past this allowed a healthy mix of offensive action against construction as well as defensive action against clearance. At Newbury the chainsaws were given five months to clear the site. Initially when protests had started the massive increased cost of clearance had pushed up costs — billed straight to the corporations, destroying any profits. Now when the contracts were tendered these millions were factored in — billed straight to the state. This made the campaigns of this period increasingly defensive in nature. Though there were attempts to move beyond this, to a certain extent it was an inevitable result of a change in 'terrain'. Yet the costs of keeping a force capable of clearing a route dotted with camps, with highly evolved defence techniques, needing highly paid specialist climbers to evict, was now immense.

Newbury, more than any other, was a national campaign in one locale. Practically everyone who had been heavily involved in radical eco stuff over the preceding five years bumped into each other in the wasteland. This was no accident — everyone knew that at Newbury the state wanted to break the movement. In reply people were determined to break the state's resolve to build roads beyond Newbury.

Glorious defeats for us meant economic defeat for the Department of Transport. This war of attrition had been rolling now for years but at Newbury both sides wanted to put in the death blow. After over a year of building defences, five months of fighting evictions, night after night of sabotage and a lifetime of manic moments, the clearance was finished; but in the aftermath so was the roads programme. Of course it took a while to die. Some projects were still in the pipeline and others were continuing, but after Newbury the conclusion was not in doubt.

A year after the clearance work had started, hundreds arrived at Newbury for the anniversary, now known as the Reunion Rampage. After minor scuffles and tedious speeches from the likes of FoE leadership, fencing surrounding a major construction compound was cut, and the crowd surged in.

So we put sand in the fuel tanks of generators, took spanners to the motor of the crane. As we were leaving the site, a tipper truck on fire to my left and the crane on fire down to my right, there was one man standing straight in front of me, silhouetted against the bright billowing flames rolling up out of the Portakabin. He stood in an X shape, his hands in victory V signs, shouting "YES! YES! YES!" It wasn't chaotic, there was a sense of purpose, of collective will, of carnival, celebration, strong magic, triumph of people power, of a small but very real piece of justice being done.[45]

After Defeats, Victories!

If this kind of disorder freaked the nation state, local government was terrified. At Guildford, Surrey Council cancelled a scheme where five camps had been set up — it simply couldn't afford the economic and social costs of taking on the movement. Opencast mines were shelved in South Wales thanks to the sterling resistance at the evictions of the Selar and Brynhennlys camps. Camps saved nature reserves from destruction by agribusiness in Sussex. Camps stopped supermarket developments. Camps stopped leisure developments in Kent, and quarries were put on hold in the Southwest after costly evictions at Dead Woman's Bottom.

If Newbury put the final nail in the coffin of the 'Roads to Prosperity' building programme, the A30 camps were shovelling in the soil. Put into full use for the first time, tunnels became another tactic of delay. Tree defence and complex subterranean networks made the eviction at Fairmile last longer than every previous eviction — with the tunnels staying occupied six days in. While the resistance to the A30 was amazing it was also a waymarker. Following the evictions there was NO daytime offensive action against the construction contract, though a one day camp and some impressive 'night-work' did get done. The amazing community had evolved over two and half years of occupation — its effect would last far longer. By mid 1997 Road Alert! could happily report the demise of the national roads programme.

It has been sliced from about £23 billion to a few £billion since 1992; nearly 500 out of the 600 road schemes have been scrapped; that's 500 places untrashed, saved — for now. These are massive cuts; Construction News wrote '...the major road-building programme has virtually been destroyed'... It seems fair to link the rise of direct action with the diminishing budget, down every year since 1993, the year of the big Twyford actions.[46]

On TV even the ex-Transport Minister Stephen Norris, of all people, presented a documentary on how 'the protesters were right' and he was wrong.

Contractor newspapers sounded more and more like obituary columns every week. The unlikely had happened, the movement's main immediate objective had been largely attained, and the "threat capacity" generated by the struggle now deterred developments in other fields. More sites were still being set up — now against disparate targets; logging in Caledonia, housing in Essex, an airport extension at Manchester.

Fly, Fly into the Streets!

While most camps were in the countryside, contestation was also spreading in the streets. After the success of the London '95 street parties, RTS followed up with an 8,000 strong take over of the M41; across the country RTSs were held in dozens of towns often more than once. Some were amazing revelatory moments — windows into future worlds — others were just crap. In '96/'97 RTS London had mobilised the alternative culture ghetto — now it was organising a break out, first making connections with the striking tube-workers, then with the locked-out Liverpool Dockers. In an inspiring act of solidarity radical eco-types climbed cranes, blockaded entrances and occupied roofs at the Docks. Around 800 protestors and dockers mingled on the action and a strong feeling of connection was born.

Following on the back of this action came a massive mobilisation just before the May election, around 20,000 marched and partied with the Dockers at the "March for Social Justice." The plan had been to occupy the then empty Department of Environment building in Whitehall. Though the police succeeded in stopping this happening, the march ended in a huge party/riot at Trafalgar Square, above the crowd a massive banner — "Never Mind the Ballots, Reclaim the Streets". More and more street parties were continuing around the country.

National Actions

After Whatley had been such a success, people wanted more. Unfortunately, the police were once bitten, twice shy. Any whiff of an EF! national mobilisation resulted in massive policing that made most actions just impossible. While the cops were still often outfoxed, mostly by moving location (an action in North Wales moved to Manchester, an action at an oil refinery moved to an open-cast site), it was largely making the best of a bad situation.

Yet it wasn't just the state that caused problems here. The big Whatley action had come out of discussion at an EF! national gathering, with groups all over committing themselves to both turning up and organising it. Other "national actions" that followed were often organised by local groups who wanted an injection of collective power into their campaign. This meant that effectively they were local campaigns calling on the national movement for support — very different from the national movement organising to support a local campaign.

One of the biggest failures came when a local group — Cardigan Bay EF! — declared a national day of action on the anniversary of the Milford Haven oil spill. This was to be followed by actions against opencast in the Welsh valleys.

Vans arrived from around the country to find little local work had been done by CBEF! (not even accommodation had been sorted) and no decent plans were in place, the "organising group" not even turning up to sort out the mess. Meanwhile hundreds of cops waited at the port. Thankfully, the wonderful Reclaim the Valleys stepped in days before they were due to and sorted a squat and a few decent actions. Nevertheless, it was a disempowering experience to say the least.

It was followed by an action at Shoreham Docks that drew 60 people... and 800 cops. Like at Milford Haven where the refinery had been closed despite no action, all work at Shoreham stopped for the day. On one level these actions were successful, in that they stopped work comprehensively, but disempowerment meant they stifled any chance of long term organising around the issue.

Public defeats also resulted in a loss to the movement "threat capacity' — something which had the power to stall developments before they started. Though even successful national actions (such as that at Doe Hill opencast in Yorkshire, which turned into a smorgasbord of criminal damage) did not result in local campaign numbers swelling, the threat capacity factor meant that local groups looked a whole lot scarier to the target involved. This fear was a factor in many developments not going ahead.

Attempts to go beyond individual land struggles to get 'at the root of the problem' usually meant taking a step backwards to occasional, media-centric events with no easily winnable immediate objectives. National direct action campaigns against the oil industry and ruling class land ownership both died early on.

A Shift from the Local to the Global

In 1997 a major shift of emphasis happened in the movement. At the time it wasn't so obvious, but after a while it would become seismic. The last massive eviction-based land struggle with multiple camps was the resistance at Manchester airport. This was near Newbury in scale and saw weeks of sieges and evictions, scraps in the trees, night-time fence pulling and underground tunnel occupations: "What Newbury did for the South, Manchester Airport did for the North in terms of attracting thousands of new people and cementing the network"[47]

Both sides of the conflict were now highly evolved, with complex delay tactics and well-trained state tunnel and tree specialists; on one level it became a clash of professionals. Manchester probably continues to have an impact on the speed at which the government is prepared to build new airports, but the campaign — unlike that against roads or quarries — was not easily reproducible. After all, there wasn't any major expansions elsewhere happening at the time.

Once the evictions had finished, some moved onto smaller camps around the country — but many of those who remained active moved off site and onto new terrains of struggle. Britain's higgeldy-piggeldy mix of land occupations, office invasions and national actions were happening in a global context, and that context was changing. In 1997 two landmark events happened, one in Cambridgeshire and one in Southern Spain; both would shape the next period.

The Mexican Zapatista rebels had inspired strugglers around the world and in 1996 held an encuentro of movements for 'land, liberty and democracy' in their Lacandon rainforest home. A diverse mix of 6,000 turned up. The following year in 1997 a second global encuentro was held in Spain. Attended by many from Britain, this proposed the formation of the Peoples' Global Action (PGA). It seemed a new global movement was being born and EF!ers wanted in. At the same time it turned out that the 'globe' was soon coming to Britain.

> In the Autumn of 1997 a handful of activists started to talk about the May 1998 G8 summit. It seemed an opportunity not to be missed — world leaders meeting in the UK and the chance to kick-start the debate on globalisation.[48]

On the continent there was increasing resistance to genetic engineering; but in Britain, none. In the summer of '97 in a potato field somewhere in Cambridgeshire activists carried out the first sabotage of a GM test site in Britain. It was the first of hundreds to come.

Land Struggles — though still useful and active — would soon no longer be the main 'hook' the movement hung on. Camps would continue to be set up and many victories (and some defeats) were yet to come but the radical ecological movement was definitely now going in a new direction. The Land Struggle Period had inspired, involved and trained thousands. Let's make no mistake — it played the major role in the cancellation of 500 new roads, numerous quarry/open cast expansions, and many house building projects. An amazing coming together of rebel subcultures (travellers, animal liberationists, EF!ers, city squatters, Welsh ex-miners, ravers, local FoE activists and the mad) forged the biggest wave of struggle for the land Industrial Britain had ever seen.

Consolidation and Global Resistance Period (1998 — 2002)

The spectacular growth of our action through much of the '90s was in part thanks to the clear ecological priority of the moment — stop roads. While many camps continued after Newbury against other developments, without the obvious and nationally unifying factor of major road-building the movement was a bit lost. We had never had to really think about what to defend before; the Department of Transport did that job for us. By moving into a period of Consolidation and Global Resistance we could pretty much sidestep this question — for a time anyway.

Throughout the '90s EF! gatherings were the main place that activists from all over got together to discuss and organise. While most that attended felt some allegiance to the EF! banner, many were not active in listed EF! groups and would not consider themselves 'EF!ers'. More, the gatherings were/are a place:

> ...where people involved in radical ecological direct action — or those who want to be — get together for four days of time and space to talk, walk, share skills, learn, play, rant, find out what's on, find out what's next, live outside, strategise, hang out, incite, laugh and conspire.[49]

At the 1997 gathering near Glasgow, attended by around 400 people in total, it was obvious that with the roads programme massively scaled down, some major things were going to change. While there were many discussions throughout the week, these were some of the key points:

🎋 The national roads programme would continue to create individual aberrations (such as Birmingham Northern Relief Road) but it would not provide so many sites for resistance nationwide.

🎋 The road campaigns had been very successful as struggles, but had largely failed to leave solid groups or communities of activists behind after the 'direct action camp roadshow' moved on.

🎋 Most of those present saw the radical ecological movement (and EF! in particular) as a network of revolutionaries, part of a global libertarian, ecological movement of movements.

Of course these things converged. Given that revolution wasn't looking immediate that week, as revolutionaries we had to be in it for 'the long haul'. The '90s had seen rapid growth, thousands had taken action but the movement, being relatively new, didn't have the infrastructure to support long term participation. With less major land struggles, less people would get involved in direct action. There was a high risk that established groups might entropy when activists got disillusioned. 'Non-aligned' individuals who had been active against roads, yet who hadn't become part of any network, might simply drift into reformist politics/work/drugs/mental asylums.[50]

Unsurprisingly the gathering didn't cook up any magical formulae, but it did throw together something passable. To tackle a drop in 'recruitment' concerted outreach would be done and to keep what activists the movement did have, local groups would consolidate. The fight against GM test sites was enthusiastically accepted as a new terrain of action.[51] The keynote evening talk on the weekend was done by a woman recently returned from the Zapatista autonomous territories. With the first congress of Peoples Global Action (PGA) coming up the following Spring it looked like despite the drop in sizeable confrontations on the land, we were in for an exciting few years...

Local Consolidation and Outreach

Squat cafés were nothing new, but 1998 saw a sudden proliferation around the country, as groups took over buildings in highly prominent locations, creating autonomous spaces where people interested in direct action could mix and conspire. In January, Manchester EF! opened up the first of many OKasional Cafés: "The squats were intended mainly to get political ideas across through socialising, as political groups in Manchester were quite inaccessible."[52]

Similar projects were carried out in Brighton, London, North Wales, Leeds, Worthing and Nottingham. In Norwich a squat café was opened because the local group "thought it would be a good idea to do a squat centre as a form of outreach and as a group building exercise."[53] In this period 'direct action forums' sprung up all over — regular town meetings for mischief making miscreants. Both the forums and the centres were essentially attempts to bring together the diverse scenes of animal liberationists, class struggle anarchists, forest gardeners, EF!ers and the like.

In parallel with this outreach, many radical eco circles were working to give themselves permanent bases and support mechanisms — needed for the long haul.[54] The number of towns with activist housing co-ops would increase substantially over the next four years. In the countryside quite a few communities of ex-road protesters would consolidate in bought or occupied land/housing from the Scottish Highlands, to Yorkshire and through to Devon. Others went onto the water in narrow boats. Following the last evictions at Manchester airport dozens moved into the Hulme redbricks in inner-city Manchester. Other needed "supports" such as vans, printing machines, a mobile action kitchen, prisoner support groups and propaganda distribution were slowly built up. This process of consolidating local direct action communities has paid a large part in making sure that the radical ecological movement hasn't been a one hit wonder: dying off after the victory against the roads programme. At its centre was the obvious truth; what's the point in trying to get more people involved if you can't keep those who already are?

On the Streets, In the Fields

This period saw an escalation of crowd action on the streets and covert sabotage in the fields: both types of action increasingly seen as part of a global struggle. In February '98 the first ever meeting of the PGA was held in Geneva, home of the World Trade Organisation (WTO). The congress, despite in-built problems, was an amazing coming together of over 300 people from movements across the globe.

> There's a woman from the Peruvian guerrilla group Tupac Amaru chatting to an Russian environmentalist. Nearby, activists from the Brazilian land squatters movement are doing some funky moves on the dancefloor with a guy from the Filipino seafarers union. Then some Brits brashly challenge a bunch of Maori indigenous activists to a drinking contest.[55]

Needless to say, the Brits lost. Ideas were swapped, arguments had and plans were laid to take action around two events coming up in May — the annual G8 meeting and the second ministerial of the WTO a day later. Back in Britain Reclaim the Streets parties were continuing around the country — Leeds' fourth RTS was typical.

> West Yorkshire coppers threatened to ruin the party before it had started, petulantly waving around side handled batons and vigorously wrestling the not-yet-inflated bouncy castle from the vigorously bouncy crowd. But after half an hour of unrest the police suddenly withdrew. Then a full on 600-strong party: bouncy castle, billowing banners, free

food and techno... At the end of the afternoon everyone escorted the system safely away, whilst the police sent a few cheeky snatch squads into the crowd's dwindling remainder; one person was run down and then beaten with truncheons. 22 arrests.[56]

Meanwhile sabotage of GM sites was on the up. The first action against a test site may have been in '97, but by the end of '98, thirty-six had been done over. Most were destroyed by small groups acting at night — covert, anonymous, prepared and loving every minute. Others were carried out by hundreds in festive daytime trashings. GM sabotage by this time was becoming an international pursuit with actions throughout the 'Global South' and trashings in four other European countries. One of the best aspects of test-site sabotage is that it has been a lot less intimidating for people to do if they have had no experience of sabotage. After all, you don't need to know your way around a JCB engine (or an incendiary device) to work out how to dig up sugar beet. Alongside sabotage, other actions against GM proliferated, ranging from office occupations to the squatting of a (recently trashed) test site.

Activists were getting more sorted, as Police Review attested: "The protesters are ingenious, organised, articulate... They use inventive tactics to achieve their aims. Forces are having to deploy increasingly sophisticated techniques in the policing of environmental protests."[57] These 'sophisticated techniques' were often quite comical: "Undercover cops who'd set up a secret camera in a Tayside farmer's barn and parked up in their unmarked car, hoping to catch some of the Scottish folk who are decontaminating their country by removing genetic test crops, had to run for their lives when the car exhaust set the barn on fire. Both the barn and the car were destroyed."[58]

On May 16th the annual G8 meeting came to Britain. The last time it had been here in 1991, half a dozen EF!ers had caused trouble. In 1998 things were a bit different — 5,000 people paralysed central Birmingham in Britain's contribution to the Global Street Party. Tripods, sound-systems and banners were all smuggled into the area.

There were some great comic scenes of police incompetence, including them surrounding the small soundsystem (disguised as a family car) and escorting it into the middle of the party. They never once asked why the 'frightened family' inside wanted to escape by deliberately driving the wrong way around the roundabout towards the crowd. By the time they realised their mistake it was all too late... the decks were under the travel blankets, boys. What threw you off the scent? The baby seat, or the toys?[59]

The party, populated by ranks of scary clowns and gurning ravers, lasted for hours, the normal strange combination of ruck and rave. Unamused, the leaders of the most powerful nations on earth fled the city for the day to a country manor. This being their showpiece, the day was a major victory.

Simultaneously other PGA affiliates were on the streets in the first International Day of Action. In India 200,000 peasant farmers called for the death of the WTO, in Brasilia, landless peasants and unemployed workers joined forces and 50,000 took to the streets. Across the world over 30 Reclaim the Streets parties took place, from Finland to Sydney, San Francisco to Toronto, Lyon to Berlin.

The world leaders flew off our island, no doubt with TV images of dancing rioters on their minds, thinking "Ah now to genteel Geneva and wine by the lake at the WTO." On arrival a huge (molotov) cocktail party welcomed them, the car of the WTO Director General was turned over and three days of heavy rioting followed. While the movement against power was always global, now it was networking and co-ordinating at a speed and depth rarely seen before.

Street parties and GM sabotage continued throughout the Summer. No longer content with holding one massive street party, RTS London organised two on the same day — in both North and South London.

By now state counter-action was a real problem; following the M41 action, the RTS office had been raided and activists arrested for conspiracy. Despite the surveillance, the parties were both pulled off beautifully, with 4,000 in Tottenham and a similar number in Brixton.

I remember two of us standing at Tottenham in the hot sun, getting drenched by a hose directed at us by a laughing local in a flat above. North London RTS had entirely outfoxed the cops and we knew so had South London. Three sound-systems, thousands of people — all blocking some of London's main arteries. It felt wonderful.

A couple of nights before, seven oil seed rape test sites had been destroyed across the country on one night. I mean, both of us were usually pretty positive about the movement, yet if a couple of years before someone had predicted that one night multiple affinity groups would covertly hit seven different targets and that that would be almost immediately followed by the simultaneous take-over of two main streets in the capital; well both of us would have thought they were a nutter. Thinking about those actions and looking around us at the smiling crowd we both cracked up, our dreams were becoming reality, we were getting stronger, the music was thumping and the party even had tented pissoirs over the drains![60]

The Struggle is Global, The Struggle is Local

The PGA International Day of Action and the Global Street Party catalysed a wave of actions across the globe, unprecedented in recent times in terms of both scale and interconnection.

Hundreds of Indian farmers from PGA affiliated organisations travelled across Europe holding meetings and demos and carrying out anti-GM actions. Strange occasions proliferated. A squatted ex-test site in Essex hosted a visit from the farmers, one of which (to much applause) sang an old Indian song about killing the English. The farmers' organisations had destroyed test sites and a laboratory in India, so despite the huge cultural differences, this was a meeting of comrades. As one Indian put it: "Together we, the peasants, and you, the poor of Europe, will fight the multinationals with our sweat and together we will succeed in defeating them." That month nine test sites were destroyed in one night and a major research organisation pulled out of GM due to being constantly attacked by direct action.[61] The year would see over 50 experiments trashed.

Next came J18, bringing actions in 27 countries by over a hundred groups. Thousands closing down the centre of the capital in Nigeria, besieging Shell, and 12,000 storming the City of London — one of the hearts of the global financial system — were just two of the highlights. J18 in London was more successful than anyone could have imagined.

Many offices were closed for the day in fear of the action. Many of those that weren't probably wished they had been. As the soundsytems played, a festive masked crowd (9,000 had been handed out) took advantage of their control of a slice of the city to dance and destroy.

> I ran into the LIFFE building [the Futures Exchange], smashing a few mirrors in the foyer and then looked round to see this masked up figure light a distress flare and hurl it up the escalators towards the offices. Fuck I thought, this is really full on. I was nicked... so I was in the police station... one cop came in drenched from head to toe in white paint. I really had to control myself to stop laughing — it looked like he'd been shat on by a huge bird.[62]

The HQ of the GM food giant Cargill had its foyer trashed as were the fronts of countless other banks, posh car showrooms and the like. The police were solidly defeated on the day. Above the crowd glittered beautiful banners, one proclaiming 'Resist, Refuse, Reclaim, Revolt'; and to back up the statement, hidden inside the banner were half a dozen broom handles — seen the next day on front covers being used against the cops to great effect. Another banner high above the street declared — 'Our Resistance is as Global as Capital', with a huge list of places where actions were happening across the planet. June 18th, more than any event before it, saw the coming together of generations of radical opposition in a celebration of our power to create another world — unified around the planet by action.

The success of the first two days of action had now created a global cycle of inspiration. In November 1999, N30 saw more action. Timed once again to coincide with the meeting of the WTO, actions happened in Britain but undoubtedly the main event was in the US — Seattle. Tens of thousands brought the city to a standstill and in three incredible days forced the meeting to close. This was understandably seen as an amazing victory, especially considering the paucity and assimilated nature of much of American opposition. The victory in America was mirrored in Britain by what many saw as a defeat. RTS London were now in a pickle. People expected them to organise big mass events, but apart from being very busy many were worried about the (violent) genie they had let out of the bottle on J18. N30 in London was a static rally, masks were not handed out. Despite the burning cop van (always a pretty sight) N30 London remained contained by the police, and to a certain extent by the organisers. For good or bad you can't turn the clock back — from now on any RTS style event in the capital would see massive policing and people coming expecting a major ruck.

Of course, resistance was not only centred around GM and the International Days of Action, or for that matter around internationalism; the local was still at the forefront for many. While the big days got the column inches, everywhere activists were fighting small local land struggles and increasingly getting stuck into community organising. In fact, in the twelve months following the Global Street Party, there were 34 direct action camps across the country.[63]

Most of these were now a combination of tree-houses, benders and tunnels and set up against a diverse set of developments. While most were populated by what The Sun described as the "tribe of treepeople," some were almost entirely done by locals — the type of people who before the 'road wars' might have simply written to their MP. Direct action was so big in the '90s that it was/is seen as a normal tactic for fighting projects. This generalisation of direct action is one of the many hidden but hugely important victories the movement has had.

While there were no major technical innovations in camps over this period (Nine Ladies in 2002 looked pretty like Manchester Airport in 1997 — but smaller) there were many victories. Simply the threat of a site stopped many developments and many camps had to "tat down" after victories, usually against local authorities or developers. Even evicted camps sometimes resulted in victory. In London a camp ran for a year against a major leisure complex in Crystal Palace Park. The eviction came at the cost of over £1 million.

> Bailiffs, accompanied by around 350 police, moved on to the site and began removing the fifty people present from the various tree and bunker defences. The eviction was completed a record breaking 19 days later when the last two occupants came out of the bunker they had been in since the beginning of the eviction.[64]

This campaign won. The eviction cost, and the prospect of more trouble, freaked out the council no end. Though this period saw far less victories than the fight against the national roads programme, it saw many more victories where camps themselves actually won there and then. Despite this, without the unifying nature of the previous period (and with many activists both "looking to the global" and not willing to go to sites), camps decreased in number.

Other factors also included increased police harassment (especially following J18) and of course "defeat through victory." In the South Downs during this time, two major developments, the Hastings Bypass and a house building project in Peacehaven[65] were both halted (for now) after direct action pledges were launched.

Many other groups have been in this situation, which, while a cause for jubilation, has meant that "the culture of camps" has suffered set-backs while its spectre wins victories. The year and a half between July '99 and January '01 saw only 10 camps operate, a quarter of the number that had been active in the previous year and a half. Since January '02 there have never been more than four ecological direct action camps at any given time.

Other local struggles such as those against casualised workplaces or for access to the land have continued, never though really become period-setting events.[66]

One major area that many have moved into — often at the same time as night-time sabotage and irregular "big days out" — has been community organising. From helping run women's refuges and self defence, to doing ecological education with kids and sorting out local food projects, this work has been an important extension of direct action.[67] While these actions don't directly defend ecologies they (hopefully) work to grow libertarian and ecological tendencies in society, an integral part of the revolutionary process.[68]

Guerrilla Gardening

The next PGA International Day of Action was Mayday 2000. Once again there were actions all over the globe. Across Britain events happened in quite a few established "activist towns," many very successfully; unfortunately overshadowing them was the mess that was the London 'Guerrilla Gardening' event.

The idea of doing another big national action was mooted at an EF! gathering in Oxford the previous winter — nearly everyone thought it a terrible concept. The state would massively prepare, the number of imprisoned activists would no doubt increase. As has been argued elsewhere,[69] Mayday 2000 — and most of its follow ups — were essentially attempts to copy J18 minus the street violence and sound-systems.

J18 had come from a momentum built up by street parties and anti-road protests, and it worked in part because it involved groups all over the country and had the element of surprise. As with national EF! actions after Whatley, the police were once bitten, twice shy. Containment of the crowd by both the cops, and in part by the organisers, created what most saw as both a rubbish party and a rubbish riot. Up until this event there had always been quite a strong 'working relationship' between radical eco groups nationwide and activists in London. Following Mayday this would, sadly decrease.

Ironically, the symbolic "guerrilla gardening" at Parliament Square only succeeded in reminding activists across the country why they liked actual guerrilla action, like covert GM sabotage; and actual gardening, on their allotments. The next year's London Mayday was hardly better. The double whammy of N30 followed by Mayday resulted in RTS London losing its 'great party' reputation, at the same time as street parties were happening less and less regularly across the country.

Meanwhile actions against GM continued to increase in scale, some involving up to 800 people. The vast majority, however, continued to be carried out covertly at night. Globally, GM sabotage was now spreading even more. Across the world shadows in the moonlight were razing GM crops trials to the ground. Spades, sticks, scythes, sickles and fire brought in the harvest. Doors splintered as labs were broken into. Pies were aimed at the arrogance of the powerful. Harassment and disruption greeted the biotech industry wherever it gathered. The deputy head of the American Treasury said in a statement to the Senate that the campaign against genetic engineering in Europe "is the greatest block to global economic liberalisation presently in existence."

The actions were hugely successful in frightening institutions into not extending GM research and forcing many supermarkets to withdraw from pushing GM food. Sadly though, "pure research" was rarely attacked in Britain. Apart from the major successes the campaign achieved/is achieving, GM sabotage schooled hundreds in covert cell-structured sabotage — a capacity which will no doubt become ever more useful.

Channel Hopping

Given the decrease in day-to-day struggle and the failure of the London street actions, there was a sharp turn towards international riot tourism. The biggest 'workshops' at the 2000 EF! Summer gathering were for those preparing to go to the next meeting of the World Bank and the IMF in Prague. Hundreds went from Britain, experiencing an exciting range of success and failure.

Divisions over violence and symbolism that were always present in the British scene were thrown into relief by the extremes of the situation. Some joined the street-fighting international black block, others (both pro- and anti- violent attacks on the summit), formed together in the Pink and Silver Block. This "Barmy Army" was a contradictory group of people with quite divergent views, pulled together by a desire for "national unity." Diversity in this case, was definitely NOT strength. Putting the problems aside (dealt with well elsewhere),[70] Prague was immensely inspiring. Thousands from all over Europe converged and forced the conferences to close early, creating a surreal, almost civil war atmosphere. Though the crowds failed to break into the conference, they shattered the desire of future cities to host these events. Previously, a visit from one of these august ruling class bodies was the dream of any town bureaucrat or politician — now it was their nightmare.

The following year, many more from the movement would go to Genoa in Italy where an unparalleled number of people on the street would clash with the state (and sometimes each other). Many also went to the anti-summit actions in Scandinavia, Switzerland and France. Only three years after the Global Street Party and the riot in Geneva started the wave of summit actions, the global elite was having to organise massive defence operations to stay safe behind their barricades. This wave of action not only inspired thousands, and spread the wildfire of resistance worldwide, it also forced many of these meetings to cut down the length of their events, move to ever less accessible fortresses and in some cases cancel their roving showcases all together.[71]

Beyond the big street spectaculars many British activists were increasingly spending time abroad, inspired by the often more up-for-it squatting scenes. This acted as a further drain on the movement, but it also brought new experiences into 'the collective mind', aided future action, made real human links across borders and just as importantly gave some amazing moments to those involved. The move to the territory of other nations, temporary for most, comes as no surprise in a period defined by its internationalism.

International Solidarity

Back in Britain, the radical ecological scene was increasingly involved in solidarity with (largely 'Third World') groups abroad. As the Malaysia campaign showed, this had always been a major part of the movement. Following the '95 EF! gathering, activists invaded a factory that built Hawk aircraft and hoisted the East Timorese flag. Throughout the land struggle period, office actions, AGM actions, embassy blockades, petrol station pickets and home visits to corporate directors had all been used to support the Ogoni/Ijaw struggle in Nigeria and the Bougainville Revolutionary Army in Papua New Guinea. Yet in this period solidarity with struggling communities beyond the capitalist core became a much bigger part of the movement. This was part and parcel of the shift in emphasis towards people seeing the radical ecological movement as part of a global revolutionary movement.

On the first business day of 1999, three groups barricaded themselves into two senior management offices and the corporate library in Shell-Mex House in London.

> January 4th was Ogoni Day, celebrated since Shell was forced out of Ogoni through massive resistance. The concerned individuals seized three key locations in the building, some of which had a pleasing view of Waterloo bridge and the banner being hung across — by others — reading "Shell: Filthy Thieving Murderers."[72]

In 1999 the keynote speech at the EF! Summer gathering was made by a visiting Papuan tribesman from the OPM. His inspirational talk resulted in actions across the country that Autumn against various corporations involved. Sporadic actions would continue in solidarity with this South Pacific struggle, as well as financial support for refugees and medical aid for prisoners, both actions which literally kept people alive.

Less theory, it was more lived experience abroad that inspired solidarity work back at home. By 2001, most towns listed with EF! groups had at least one returnee from the jungles of the Mexican South West. In 2001 a steady stream of activists going to Palestine started, many doing valuable on-the-ground solidarity work in the heat of the second Intifada — and the Israeli crackdown.

Those returning from abroad wanted to "bring the war home" with a range of actions, speaking tours and fundraising pushes. Of course GM actions are also in part solidarity actions with Third World peasants. From benefit gigs to demos at the Argentinian embassy — solidarity work was increasingly filling the gap a lack of land struggles left behind.

Then and Now

This decade-long retrospective ends at the end of 2001, nevertheless I'll say a little about where we find ourselves. Looking at the first EF! AU of 2002, it seems strange, slightly worrying, but also inspiring that 10 years on there is an obvious continuity of action through the decade: a new protest site, night-time sabotage actions, actions against summits, anti-war demos. The centre spread is a briefing for the campaign to defend Northern peat bogs, a struggle from right back in 1991 (and further) that re-started in 2001 and is covered elsewhere in this issue.

In a way the last year or so has reminded me of the film *Back to the Future* (now I'm showing my age); not only was the peat campaign back up and running, but also there was an anti-road gathering in Nottingham, and actions were announced to aid tribal groups in the Pacific.

There are now far fewer EF! groups listed than in the mid '90s, and the travelling culture many site activists came from has been largely destroyed by state force and drugs. Nevertheless, the radical ecological movement is in a surprisingly healthy state and has succeeded in not being assimilated into the mainstream. Ten years on and we're still more likely to be interviewed by the police than a marketing consult or academic (remember to say "No Comment" to all three!). The movement is still active and still raw. Many places continue to be saved by ecological direct action, our threat potential still puts the willies up developers, and people are still getting involved and inspired.

Our gathering this year will probably be attended by around 350-400 in total — the same kind of number it has been since 1996. While we don't want to build up the movement like a Leninist party — 'more members, please more members'— the fact that we have stayed at this number despite catalysing situations of struggle involving thousands should give us some pause for thought.

Two prime contradictions have haunted the radical ecological resistance on this island. British EF! was born as a wilderness defence movement with no wilderness, and evolved into a network of revolutionaries in non-revolutionary times.

The process of consolidation that was started in 1997 enabled radical ecological circles to survive the slowdown of domestic land struggles after the victory against national roadbuilding. This process combined with the upsurge in "global resistance" enabled us in part to side-step the questions posed by the above contradictions.

If we want to see the wildlands defended and any chance of libertarian, ecological (r)evolution increase then practical action is needed. Much is already underway, but more is needed and without a clear strategy we are bound to fail.

On a personal note the "10 years of radical ecological action" documented here have been immensely inspiring to me. It's been an honour to stand on the front lines (as well as lounge about in lounges) with some lovely, brave, insightful and amazing people.

Thank you.

BIBLIOGRAPHIES

Brian Morris

Angus, I (2016) Facing the Anthropocene

Berry, T (1988) The Dream of the Earth

Biehl, J (1998) The Politics of Social Ecology: Libertarian Municipalism, (2015) Ecology or Catastrophe: The Life of Murrary Bookchin

Black, B (1997) Anarchy After Leftism

Bookchin, M (1971) Post-Scarcity Anarchism, (1980) Toward an Ecological Society, (1982) The Ecology of Freedom, (1986) The Modern Crisis, (1989) Social Ecology vs Deep Ecology, (1989) Remaking Society, (1992) Urbanization Without Cities, (1995) The Philosophy of Social Ecology, (1995) Re-Enchanting Humanity, (1995) Social Anarchism or Lifestyle Anarchism (1999) Anarchism, Marxism and the Failure of the Left

Curry, P (2011) Ecological Ethics: An Introduction

Dawkins, Richard (1976) The Selfish Gene

Devall, B and C (1985) Deep Ecology

Dubos, R (1968) So Human an Animal

Eiglad, E (2014) Communalism an Alternative

Ekins, P (1992) The New World Order

Engels, F (1940) The Dialectics of Nature (1969) Anti-Duhring

Foster, E (2000) Marx's Ecology: Materialism and Nature

Fromm, E (1949) Man For Himself

Goodwin, B (1994) How the Leopard Changed its Spots

Gore, A (2009) Our Choice: A Plan to Solve the Cliimate Crisis

Kovel, J (2002) The Enemy of Nature

Kropotkin, Peter (1902) Mutual Aid

Lamont C (1949) The Philosophy of Humanism

Latour, B (2017) Facing Gaia

Lehning, Arthur (1973) Michael Bakunin's Selected Writings

Manes,C (1990) Green Rage

Mangulis, L (1981) Symbiosis in Cell Evolution

Marshall, P (1992) Demanding the Impossible

McKay, I (2007) Murray Bookchin (1921-2006) in Anarcho-Syndicalist Review

Monbiot, G (2006) Heat: How to Stop The Planet Burning

Morris, B (1996) Ecology and Anarchism, (2004) Kropotkin: The Politics of Community, (2012) Pioneers of Ecological Humanism, Anthropology and the Human Subject, (2014) Anthropology, Ecology and Anarchism: A Reader, Mumford, Lewis (1952) The Conduct of Life

Naess, A (1989) Ecology, Community and Lifestyle
Nasr, S H (1996) Religion and the Order of Nature
Price, A (2012) Recovering Bookchin
Radkau, J (2014) The Age of Ecology: A Global History
Roussopoulos, D (2015) Political Ecology: Beyond Environmentalism
Scruton, R (2012) Green Philosophy
Sears, P (1964) Ecology, a Subversive Science
Starhawk (1979) The Spiral Dance
Tudge, C (2016) Sic Steps Back to the Land
Watson, D (1996) Beyond Bookchin, (1999) Against the Megamachine

Chris Wilbert

AFRC Institute of Horticultural Research — (1988) East Mailing 1913–88 75th anniversary brochure.
AFRC Institute of Horticultural Research — (1988) Annual Report 1988 Berry, Wendell — (1966) The Broken Ground Cape.
Bianchini, F et al — (1975) The Complete Book of Fruits and Vegetables New York, Crown.
Blythe, R — (1968) Akenfield Penguin.
Braverman, H. (1974) Labor and Monopoly Capital Monthly Review Press.
Cantor, L. (1987) The Changing English Countryside 1400–1700 Routledge and Kegan
Clutterbuck, C. and Lang, T. (1982) More Than We Can Chew Pluto Press
Cooper, J.C. (1978) An Illustrated Encyclopaedia of Traditional Symbols Thames and Hudson.
Courtney, M.A. (1973) Cornish Feasts and Folklore EP Publishing.
Douglas, J.D. (Editor) (1962) The New Bible Dictionary Intervarsity Press.
Flaherty, Ann (1989) Uniroyal Pushed into Suspending Alar Sales in US Grower 15.6.1989 p4.
Flaherty, Ann (1989) Alar Cleared of Health Risk by the Governments ACP Grower 21.12.1989 p4.
Fräser, J.G. (1949) The Golden Bough MacMillan.
Graves, R. (1952) The White Goddess Third Edition, Faber and Faber.
Greenoak, F. (1983) Forgotten Fruit Andre Deutsch.
Harman, C. (1989) From Feudalism to Capitalism International Socialism 45 Winter 1989 pp35-88.
Harvey, David (1973) Fruit Growing in Kent in the Nineteenth Century in: Roake, M. and Whyman, J. Essays in Kentish History Frank Cass.
Herrsher, Pascal (1988) Death of the European Landscape? Environmental Conservation Vol 15 (1) Spring 1988 pp63-4.
Hill, L.D. (1974) Grow Your Own Fruit and Vegetables Faber and Faber. Hobsbawm, E.J.

130

and Rude, G. (1968) Captain Swing Norton and Co. Horticultural Product News (1989) Compact Apple Trees May 1989 p24. Hughes, J.D. (1975) Ecology in Ancient Civilisations University of New Mexico. Hull, Eleanor (1928) Folklore of the British Isles Methuen.

Jackson, A.A. (1973) Semi-Detached London Allen and Unwin.

Jones, Alwyn (1983) Beyond Industrial Society: Towards Balance and Harmony The Ecologist Vol 13 (4) ppl4I-147.

Jordan, W.K. (1973) Social Institutions in Kent 1480–1660: A Study of Social Aspirations in: Roake, M. and Whyman Essays in Kentish History Frank Cass.

Lawson, G. (1989) Automated Spraying Grower 23.11.1989 p26.

Luckwill, L.C. (1984) Some Factors in Successful Cropping 5 Apple Span 27 (2) p66.

Mabey, R. and Greenoak, F. (1983) Back to the Roots Arena.

McCully, P. and Hildyard (1989) Intolerable Risks: Pesticides in Children's Food The Ecologist Vol 19(3) p97.

Merchant, Carolyn (1982) The Death of nature Wildwood House. Morris, B. (1981) Changing Views of nature The Ecologist Vol 11(3) ppl31-8. Newby, Howard (1979) Green and Pleasant Land Wildwood House. Newby, Howard (1987) Country Life Cardinal.

Prothero, R.E. (1917) English Farming Past and Present Second Edition, Longmans, Green and Co.

Roach, F.A. (1985) Cultivated Fruits of Britain Blackwell.

Robinson, G.M. (1988) Agricultural Change North British Publishers.

Rothenberg, D. (Editor) and Naess, A. (1989) Ecology, Community and Lifestyle C.U.P.

Russell, Claire (1981) The Life Tree and the Death Tree Folklore Vol 92(1) pp56-62.

Sinden, Neil (1989) Orchards and Places in: Orchards a Guide to Local Conservation Common Ground.

Snell, Peter (1989) Pesticide Residues: The Scandal Continues The Ecologist Vol 19(3) pp94-97.

Talbot White, J. (1984) Country London Routledge and Kegan Paul.

Thomas, Keith (1983) Man and the Natural World: Changing Attitudes in England 1500–1800 Allen Cane.

Tisdell, C.A. (1989) Environmental Conservation: Economics, Ecology and Ethics Environmental Conservation Vol 16(2) ppl07-12.

Walters, A.H. (1973) Ecology, Food and Civilisation: an Ecological History of Human Society Knight.

Ward, R. (1988) A Harvest of Apples Penguin.

Weldon-Finn, R. (1973) The Domesday Book: A Guide Phillimore and Co. Wicks, J.H. (1972) Trees of the British Isles in History and Legend Anchor Press.

REFERENCEJ & NOTEJ

a polemic on ecology

1. George Bradford 1989 How Deep is Deep Ecology, Hadley, Mass. Times Change Press.

2. Murray Bookchin 1989 Remaking Society, Montreal, Black Rose Books. 1990 The Philosophy of social ecology Montreal, Black Rose Books.

3. David Levine 1991 Ed. Defending the Earth, A Dialogue between Murray Bookchin and Dave Foreman.

4. Bill Devall 1988 Simple in Means, Rich in Ends: Practicing Deep Ecology Salt Lake City, Peregrine Smith.

5. Arne Naess 1989 Ecology, Community and Lifestyle Cambridge Univ. Press.

6. Hans Jonas 1966 The Phenomenon of Life Univ. Chicago Press.

7. Sinden, Neil — "Orchards and Places" in Orchards: A Guide to Local Conservation Common Ground 1989 p1O.

8. Merchant, Carolyn — The Death of nature: Women, Ecology and the Scientific Revolution London Wildwood House 1982 p43.

9. Clutterbuck, C and Lang, T — More Than We Can Chew: The Crazy World of Food and Farming Pluto Press 1982 p66.

10. Tisdell, C A — Environmental Conservation: Economics, Ecology and Ethics, Environmental Conservation Vol 16 No 2 Summer 1989 p107.

11. Berry Wendell — The Broken Ground Cape 1966 p31.

12. Hills L D — Grow Your Own Fruit and Vegetables Faber and Faber 1974 p203.

13. Bianchini F et al — The Complete Book of Fruits and Vegetables New York Crown 1975 pi 26.

14. Walters AH — Ecology, Food and Civilisation: An Ecological History of Human Society London Knight 1973 p20.

15. Greenoak F — Forgotten Fruit Andre Deutsch 1983 p3.

16. Weldon — Finn, R — The Domesday Book: A Guide Sussex Phillimore and Co 1973 p59.

17. Cooper J C — An Illustrated Encyclopaedia of Traditional Symbols Thames and Hudson 1978 p176.

18. Hull, Eleanor — Folklore of the British Isles London Methuen 1928 p22.

19. Morris, B — Changing View of nature The Ecologist Vol 11(3. 1981 p131.

20. Merchant, C — Op Cit p3.

21. Hull, Eleanor — Op Cit p240.

22. Morris, B — Op Cit p131.

23. Douglas J D (Editor. — The New Bible Dictionary Intervarsity Press 1962 p50.

24. Russell, Claire — The Life Tree and the Death Tree Folklore Vol 92(i. 1981 p56.

25. Ibid p56-7.

26. Cooper, J C — Op Cit p14.

27. Ibid.

28. Fräser, J G — The Golden Bough Abridged Edition MacMillan 1949

29. Hull, E — Op Cit p22.

30. Graves, Robert — The White Goddess 3rd edition Faber and Faber 1952 p42.

31. Hull, E — Op Cit p240.

32. Roach, F A — Cultivated Fruits of Britain Blackwell 1985 p1OO.

33. Hull, E — Op Cit p227 and p240.

34. Wicks, J H — Trees of the British Isle in History and Legend Essex Anchor Press 1972 pi 22.

Courtney, M A — Cornish Feasts and Folklore Yorkshire E P Publishing 1973 p9.

35. Wicks, J H — Op Cit p122.

36. Fräser, J G — Op Cit p682.

37. Merchant, C — Op Cit p43.

38. Ibid p78.

39. Ibid p43.

40. Harman, C — From Feudalism to Capitalism International Socialism 45 Winter 1989 (p35-88. p37.

41. Merchant, C — Op Cit p52.

42. Thomas, Keith — Man and the Natural World: Changing Attitudes in England 1500–1800 Allen Lane 1983 p253.

43. Roach, F A — Op Cit p34.

44. Hughes, J Donald — Ecology in Ancient Civilisations Univ of New Mexico US p29.

45. Greenoak, F — Op Cit p3.

46. Talbot-White, J — Country London Routledge and Kegan Paul 1984 p2I.

47. Roach, F A — Op Cit p22.

48. Ibid p22.

49. Ibid p24.

50. Robinson, G M — Agricultural Change Edinburgh North British Pub. 1988 p96.

51. Cantor, Leonard — The Changing English Countryside 1400–1700 Routledge and Kegan Paul 1987 p56.

52. Jordan, W K — Social Institutions in Kent 1480–1660: A Study of the Changing Patterns of Social Aspirations in Roake, M and Whyman, J (editors. — Essays in Kentish History London Frank Cass 1973 p85.

53. Roach, F A — Op Cit p48.

54. Ibid p91.

55. Thomas, Keith — Op Cit p256.

56. Ibid p256

57. Roach, F A — Op Cit p59

58. Newby, Howard — Country Life: A Social History of Rural England Cardinal 1987 p6.

59. Hobsbawm, E J & Rude, G — Captain Swing Norton and Co 1968 p 27.

60. Harvey, David — Fruit Growing in Kent in the Nineteenth Century in Essays in Kentish History Op Cit p214-6.

61. Roach, F A — Op Cit p95.

62. Ibid p65.

63. Ibid p69-72.

64. Braverman, Harry — Labor and Monopoly Capital London Monthly Review Press 1964 pi 56.

65. Ibid p256.

66. Jones, Alwyn — Beyond Industrial Society: Towards Balance and Harmony, The Ecologist Vol 13(4. 1983 pi42.

67. Braverman, Harry — Op Cit p171.

68. Newby, Howard — Green and Pleasant Land? Wildwood House 1979 p75.

69. AFRC Institute of Horticultural Research — East Mailing 1913–88 1988 p13.

70. Ibid p3.

71. This is based on reviews of horticultural product magazines and on personal communications with East Mailing and Fruit Growers. There is a move towards integrated pest control but this is developing only slowly.

72. McCully, P and Hildyard, N — Intolerable Risks: Pesticides in Children's Food The Ecologist Vol 19(3. 1989 p97.

73. Snell, Peter — Pesticide Residues: The Scandal Continues The Ecologist Vol 19(3. 1989 p94.

74. Flaherty, Ann — Uniroyal Pushed into Suspending Alar Sales in US Grower 15.6.1989 p4.

75. Flaherty, Ann — Alar Cleared of Health Risk by the Governments ACP Grower 21.12.1989 p4.

76. Luckwill, L C — Some Factors in Successful Cropping 5 Apples Span 27(2. 1984 p66.

77. Lawson, G — Automated Spraying Grower 23.11.1989 p26.

78. East Mailing 1913–88 Op Cit p15.
AFRC Institute of Horticultural Research — Annual Report 1988 p32.

79. Compact Apple Trees — Horticultural Product News May 1989 p24.

80. Mabey, R and Greenoak, F — Back to the Roots Arena 1983 p85.

81. Sinden, Neil — "Orchards and Places" Op Cit p8-9.

82. Prothero, R E — English Farming Past and Present second edition, London, Longmans, Green and Co 1917.

83. Herrscher, Pascall — Death of the European Landscape? ENV Conservation Vol 15(1. Spring 1988 p63-4.

84. Blythe, Ronald — Akenfield Penguin 1969 Chapter 12. This information is based on several interviews undertaken in 1988–89 in large commercial orchards in North Kent and

so cannot be taken as representative of all orchard works.

85. Cooper, J C — Op Cit p7.

86. Jackson, A A — Semi-Detached London Allen and Unwin 1973 pi49.

87. Ibid pi50.

88. Ward, R — A Harvest of Apples Penguin 1988 p16.

89. Personal correspondence with Neil Sinden from Common Ground.

90. Alexander, C et al — A Pattern Language, Towns, Buildings, Construction O.U.P. 1977 p795.

91. Tisdell, C A — Op Cit p107.

92. Jones, Alwyn — Op Cit p142.

93. Rothenberg, D (Editor. in: Naess, A — Ecology, Community and Lifestyle O.U.P. 1989 p2.

94. Alexander, C — Op Cit p795.

95. Appleyard, D — Urban Trees, Urban Forest: What Do They Mean? in: Hopkins, G (Editor. Proc. of the National Urban Forestry Conference I Nov. 13–16 1978. Washington DC Suny College of Env. Science and Forestry Syracuse NY (pp 138–155. p144.

96. Sinden, N — "Conserving Fruit Trees — Op Cit p40.

97. Cooper, J C — Op Cit p 132.

after thought, action

1. The Ecologist, Vol. 2, No. 12, December 1972

2. Eco-Warriors by Rik Scarce, (ISBN 0 9622683 3 X., p. 103

3. Green Rage, Christopher Manes, p. 65

4. Speech by Dave Foreman, Grand Canyon, 7/7/87

5. FoE Newsletter No. 1, Jan 1972

6. While FoE and GP remain centrist, both groups increasingly try to engage their membership AS activists not just as supporters. This, as many of their staff admit, is due to the influence of the '90s land struggles.

7. A ridiculous statement I admit — but true!

8. Direct Action Video, Oxford EF!

9. 'Militancy', FoE Newsletter, No. 10, Oct 1972

10. EF! Action Update, No. 3

11. Ibid.

12. Noticibly South Somerset EF! who organised the early Whatley Quarry actions.

13. This description is no joke — one described herself on more than one occasion as 'the queen of the tribe'!

14. Dept of Transport Affidavit concerning May 1st 1993

15. Welcome Back Twyford Six, Do or Die No. 3, p. 45

16. 'Car Chases, Sabotage and Arthur Dent: Twyford Diary', Pt. 2, Do or Die, No. 3, p. 21

17. Ibid., p. 22

18. 'Skye Campaign Soaked in Sea of Anger', Do or Die, No. 3, p. 11

19. EF! Action Update, No. 5

20. 'For Flapjack and Mother Earth: Earth Warriors At Jesmond Dene', www.eco-action. org/dt/jesmond.html

21. Ibid.

22. 'News From The Autonomous Zones', Do or Die No. 4, p. 21

23. Ibid., p. 22

24. Ibid., p. 23

25. These were not police smear stories. There was only a few sentences ever mentioning them and no tabloid 'eco-terrorist' horror stories. If anything the state probably enforced a 'quieting strategy' on the situation as they did to the ALF at its height of support.

26. Copse: The Cartoon Book of Tree Protesting by Kate Evans, (ISBN 0 9532674 07., p. 32

27. EF! Action Update, No. 9

28. Copse, p. 20

29. 'Leadenham', Do or Die No. 4, p. 6

30. Fash threatened a number of sites through the '90s. At Jesmond they were chased off, running for their lives (which is what they do best. — mostly they didn't even turn up (with the one major exception of the M11.. Far more dangerous were random individual loonies. Arson attacks on camps happened right from the beginning — both at Twyford and the M11. Of course the police paid little notice. On one occasion when some posh student arsonists were nicked at Newbury (after they had put a petrol bomb through a truck window and into a sleeping child's bedroom. they got off — the magistrates viewed them as drunken pranksters.

31. Daily Post (North Wales., 9/1/94

32. Green Anarchist was undoubtedly a great influence on this period. One big gripe though — again and again one would read GA reports of actions which said the Earth Liberation Front had done this or that. Some may have been true but most of these claimed actions were often simply done by crowds or 'camp warparties'. In fact on a number of occasions people have been arrested for criminal damage only to read later in GA that 'the ELF' had carried out their action. This is both dishonest and dangerous.

33. Jonathan Dimbelby at Solsbury Hill for instance.

34. Construction News

35. 'The Battle For Hyde Park: Ruffians, Radicals and Ravers, 1855-1994', (Practical History.

36. 'CJB: Business As Usual', EF! Action Update, No. 12

37. Schnews, No. 3

38. 'London Regional Report', Do or Die, No. 5, p. 23

39. Ibid., p. 25

40. 'Meanwhile Down in the West-Country', Do or Die, No. 5, p. 18

41. 'It's (Not Really That. Grim Up North!', Do or Die, No. 5, p. 12

42. EF! Action Update, No. 23

43. Thames Valley Police Press Release 11/11/96

44. Copse, p. 105

45. There's A Riot Going On by Merrick (Godhaven Press.

46. 'Direct Action, Six Years Down the Line', Do or Die, No. 7, p. 1

47. EF! Action Update, No. 40

48. Global Street Party — Birmingham and the G8, p. 3

49. EF! Summer Gathering 2003 leaflet.

50. This reference to Mental Asylums is no joke — over a dozen people were sectioned from Newbury alone, prompting the setting up of the 'Head State Support Group'. Land Struggles had been immensely therapeutic for many, but for some they became the catalyst for mental breakdown. On sites the intense connection to other people and the land was amazing. Feeling the land being ripped all around you and having your community broken up was unbearable for many. Some would have been broken by Industry either way, but it was the movement's duty to provide support for those who were asked to risk all. It mostly failed in that duty.

51. It's worth pointing out that EF! is a network of autonomous groups and individuals. Gatherings can be the place where people decide what they are going to do, but they cannot decide what others should or shouldn't do. After a number of bad experiences with people representing the movement in outside publications and stating that 'EF! has said the...' it was decided that gatherings would mostly not distribute written reports — too often the writer's own political dogma misrepresented the consensus — or lack of one. Here, I am trying to sum up some of the points the '97 gathering came up with in consensus. I have asked around to check that my memory is correct, but I may too have clouded the reality of the discussion with the fog of my own particular dogma. I apologise if this is so.

52. 'Autonomous Spaces', Do or Die No. 8, p. 130

53. Ibid.

54. Fears that the giro checks would soon stop arriving, bringing an end to the dole autonomy that, along with student grants and crime, had been the main economic backbone of movements here for generations was also a major factor. Resistance to the introduction of the Jobseekers Allowance and the New Deal did occur — but with most claimants not joining in with collective efforts to repel the squeeze, the campaign was doomed. By individualising their problem people were collectively defeated.

55. Schnews, No. 156

56. Schnews, No. 167

57. Police Review, quoted in 'Surveillance Watch', Schnews Survival Handbook

58. EF! Action Update, No. 50

59. Global Street Party: Birmingham and the G8 pamphlet.

60. The reference — me and a mate on a glorious day!

61. EF! Action Update, No. 59

62. 'Friday June 18th 1999: Confronting Capital and Smashing the State', Do or Die No. 8, p. 20

63. 'Carry on Camping', Do or Die No. 8, p. 148

64. EF! Action Update, No. 57

65. EF! Action Update, No. 48

66. For a short while it looked like The Land Is Ours might successfully set off a wave of action around the country. However the entrenched nature of the problem and the spectacular, media-centric style of some of the main 'occupations' cut that possibility short.

67. There is always a danger here of merely becoming unpaid social workers. For too many in the past community organising has been a way back into the mainstream. That this is a danger should not stop people doing these bread and butter activities — but should remind us to be ever vigilant against assimilation.

68. One argument put forward for community organising over ecological defence, is that only the working class can defeat capitalism so 'real work' needs to be done 'in' the working class to strengthen 'it' and radicalise it. Apart from the obvious patronising missionary attitude this view ignores the fact that the Land Struggle Period saw large actions with and by working class communities across the country; a level of joint action most traditional class struggle anarchos could only dream of. While many of the places '90s land struggles happened in were 'Tory shires' others were in the old 'barracks of the labour movement' — the East End, South Wales, Glasgow, inner-city Manchester and the Yorkshire mining areas!

69. For a good analysis of this debacle see — 'May Day: Guerrilla? Gardening?', Do or Die No. 9, p. 69

70. 'Here Comes the Barmy Army!', Do or Die No. 9, p. 12

71. This year's EU summit in Greece is likely to be the last outside of the EU Fortress in Brussels.

72. EF! Action Update, No. 55 The oldest anarchist publishing house in the English speaking world,

ALSO FROM FREEDOM...

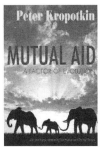